FASAB

Federal Accounting Standards Advisory Board

DISCUSSION PAPER

ACCOUNTING FOR THE NATURAL RESOURCES OF THE FEDERAL GOVERNMENT

PREPARED BY

THE FASAB NATURAL RESOURCES TASK FORCE

THIS DOCUMENT IS NOT CONSIDERED AUTHORITATIVE AND SHOULD BE USED FOR DISCUSSION PURPOSES ONLY

June 2000

THE FEDERAL ACCOUNTING STANDARDS ADVISORY BOARD

The Federal Accounting Standards Advisory Board (the FASAB or "the Board") was established by the Secretary of the Treasury, the Director of the Office of Management and Budget (OMB), and the Comptroller General in October 1990. It is responsible for promulgating accounting standards for the United States Government.

An accounting standard is typically formulated initially as a proposal after considering the financial and budgetary information needs of citizens (including the news media, state and local legislators, analysts from private firms, academe, and elsewhere), Congress, Federal executives, Federal program managers, and other users of Federal financial information. The proposed standard is published in an Exposure Draft for public comment. A public hearing is sometimes held to receive oral comments in addition to written comments. The Board considers comments and decides whether to adopt the proposed standard with or without modification. The Board publishes adopted standards in a Statement of Federal Financial Accounting Standards.

Additional background information is available from the FASAB:

"Memorandum of Understanding among the General Accounting Office, the Department of the Treasury, and the Office of Management and Budget, on Federal Government Accounting Standards and a Federal Accounting Standards Advisory Board," amended on October 1, 1999.

"Mission Statement of the Federal Accounting Standards Advisory Board."

Federal Accounting Standards Advisory Board

441 G Street, NW, Suite 6814
Washington, DC 20548
Telephone (202) 512-7350
Fax (202) 512-7366
www.financenet.gov/fasab.htm

Executive Summary

During the Board's deliberations relating to the development of an accounting standard for land, natural resources were excluded from the scope of the land project. Accordingly, the Board established a Natural Resources task force to address natural resources separately. On the basis of the guidance provided by the Board, the task force was charged to: (1) study the kinds of information (i.e., both financial data and nonfinancial data) which can be reported about natural resources, (2) provide options for reporting the information, (3) identify the related impacts on existing FASAB standards based on the options and, (4) identify existing laws and regulations that affect reporting information about natural resources. This report presents the findings of the task force based on its charge.

The report contains the following major sections:

- I.   Natural Resources Project Overview
- II. Objectives of Natural Resources Reporting
- III. Context for Analysis -- Framework
- IV. General Reporting Principles
- V.   Implication of Recommendations
- VI. Indian Natural Resource Assets
- Appendix A. Reporting by Individual Resource
- Appendix B. Minority Comments on General Reporting Principles

An overview of the sections is provided below:

Section I, *Natural Resources Project Overview*, provides an overview of how various aspects of the project were developed, as well as, the scope of the project. The Board provided the scope in which the task force would focus its work. The scope included economic mineral resources (e.g., oil, gas, coal, gold, silver, copper, sand, clay, and gravel); the following renewable resources: timber, forage, and water for which the Federal Government owned the rights; and the electromagnetic spectrum.

Section II, *Objectives of Natural Resources Reporting*, outlines the reporting objectives the task force used in developing the report. As its basis, the task force used Statement of Federal Financial Accounting Concept Statement (SFFAC) No. 1, *Objectives of Federal Financial Reporting*, to ensure that all of the major objectives were considered. The report specifically focuses on the premise that natural resource reporting can report on past performance from a budgetary, operating, or stewardship perspective. In this section it is noted that natural resource reporting could also serve natural resources accounting by providing information relevant to policy decisions about the future management and the disposition of Federal natural resources.

Section III of the report, *Context for Analysis -- Framework*, was developed by the task force to provide a framework for understanding how the many Federal natural resource programs are managed. This understanding became necessary as the task force began to discuss natural resource reporting options. This section also discusses the following natural resource management processes:

- undiscovered resources
- resources not available for transfer
    - -- legislatively withdrawn resources
    - -- administratively withdrawn resources
- resources available for transfer
    - -- resources planned to be offered
    - -- resources under contract but not conveyed
    - -- other available resources
- conveyed.

Section IV, *General Reporting Principles,* gives detailed discussions on the various reporting options considered by the task force. It addresses asset reporting, accounting and reporting for revenue, and accounting and reporting for cost. The task force's suggested reporting principles, as well as, advantages and disadvantages of these principles are presented for 1) asset reporting and 2) accounting and reporting for cost. However, the accounting and reporting for revenue discussion was heavily debated and a consensus was not reached on a suggested reporting principle. Therefore, two revenue accounting and reporting options have been provided.

The asset reporting segment outlines the various reporting options for reporting natural resource assets on the financial statements (i.e., recognition, disclosure, and stewardship reporting). Based on it findings, the task force agreed that stewardship reporting could be used as the primary tool for reporting natural resource information. The two revenue accounting and reporting options are 1) reporting all natural resource revenues on the Statement of Custodial Activities and, 2) reporting all natural resource revenues on the Statement of Net Costs. The accounting and reporting for cost section is divided into the following cost segments: cost of resources, cost of sale, cost of management, and transfer of revenue/distribution of receipts.

Section V, *Implication of Recommendations*, focuses on the implications of the task force's suggested reporting principles and revenue options on SFFAS No. 7, *Accounting for Revenue and Other Financing Sources and Concepts for Reconciling Budgetary and Financial Accounting* and the legal/regulatory statutes to be considered.

Section VI, *Indian Natural Resource Assets*, provides information on Indian natural resource assets from the standpoint of these assets being reported as trust assets. This section also provides an overview of FASAB Interpretation No. 1, *Interpretation of Federal Financial Accounting Standards -- Reporting on Indian Trust Funds in General Purpose Financial Reports of the Department of the Interior and in the Consolidated Financial Statements of the United States Government: an Interpretation of SFFAS No. 7.*

Appendix A, *Reporting by Individual Resource*, contains detailed information on eight natural resources related programs managed by the Federal Government. They are as follows:

- timber,
- outer continental shelf oil and gas,
- leasable minerals (solid),
- leasable minerals (fluid),
- locatable minerals,
- mineral materials,
- grazing uses , and
- electromagnetic spectrum (airwaves).

Appendix B, *Minority Comments on General Reporting Principles*, raises three concerns. First, it suggests that the basic concepts of SFFAS No. 7 are valid, and that sales of natural resources should not offset agencies' gross costs, unless the full costs of the natural resources sold are recognized. Second, it suggests that some natural resource assets -- in particular, those where the asset is held for remunerative operations or sale -- should be recognized on the balance sheet, and not solely in the stewardship report; this would also allow the full costs of natural resources that are sold to be recognized on the Statement of Net Cost. Finally, the comments suggest that the Federal Government develop basic data where it has valuable resources that it intends to sell or manage for remunerative purposes.

TABLE OF CONTENTS

FASAB NATURAL RESOURCES TASK FORCE MEMBERS

R. Schuyler Lesher, Task Force Chairman
Department of the Interior

H. Theodore Heintz, Jr.
Department of the Interior

Robert Anderson
Bureau of Land Management

Buddy Arvizo
Bureau of Land Management

Emil Attanasi, Economist
US Geological Survey

Jack Blickley
US Geological Survey

Christine Bonham
US General Accounting Office

Betty Buxton
Bureau of Land Management

Debra Carey
Department of the Interior

Mike Chatmon
Department of the Interior

Walter Cruickshank
Minerals Management Service

Edward Darragh
USDA - U.S. Forest Service

William deBardelaben
Department of Defense

Jim Handlon
Bureau of Reclamation

George Keller
Minerals Management Service

Allan Lund
Department of the Treasury

Randy Lyon
Office of Management & Budget

James Mobley
USDA - U.S. Forest Service

Robert Myers
Department of Energy

Jose Oyola
US General Accounting Office

Clyde Topping
Bureau of Land Management

Robert Repetto
World Resources Institute

Monica R. Valentine
Federal Accounting Standards Advisory Board

Richard Wascak
Federal Accounting Standards Advisory Board

William Woodson
Department of Defense - Army

I. Natural Resources Project Overview

Background

In earlier deliberation by the Federal Accounting Standards Advisory Board (FASAB) on Property, Plant, and Equipment (SFFAS No. 6) and Supplementary Stewardship Reporting (SFFAS No. 8), the land was defined as the solid part of the surface of the earth. For the purpose of those standards, natural resources that are in the custody of the Federal Government were excluded from the scope of the land project. The major reasons for addressing only surface land in the previous standards were: (1) the allotted time frame within which to complete the standard for land; (2) studies that pointed out the difficulties and complexities of accurately estimating and valuing natural resources; and (3) disputes regarding the boundaries of the outer-continental shelf.

As a follow-up effort, the Board established a Natural Resources Project task force to address natural resources separately. The purpose of the task force was to provide the framework for the development of a natural resources accounting standard.

The responsibilities assigned to the task force to accomplish this task were:

1) Study the kinds of information about extractable natural resources owned by the Federal Government, or under Federal stewardship, which can be obtained for reporting purposes, including information about the value of resources removed, what was received in exchange, the cost of allowing the resources to be taken, and the value of resources remaining;

2) Provide options for reporting information in an annual report, i.e., on face of the financial statements, in footnotes, as required supplemental stewardship information (RSSI), as required supplemental information (RSI), or in the Management Discussion and Analysis (MD&A); and

3) Identify areas in existing FASAB standards that would be impacted by the task force's recommended reporting options, and the required changes to the standards associated with each option.

In addition, the task force was asked to identify existing laws and regulations that affect the ability of the Federal Government to properly report on these natural resources to the extent that these laws and regulations were noted during the course of the study.

Scope

The task force was requested to address "traditional" natural resources associated with Federal lands. In addition, stocks of game, fisheries, and wildlife habitat were specifically excluded from the scope of the project.

The task force proposed to focus on extractable natural resources owned by the Federal Government, or under Federal stewardship, for which a commercial market existed for the resource. The revised scope included economic mineral resources (e.g., oil, gas, coal, gold, silver, copper, sand, clay, and gravel); the following renewable resources: timber, forage, and water for which the Federal Government owned the rights; and the electromagnetic spectrum. However, as the project progressed, the focus of the task force shifted from a commercial market orientation to a stewardship orientation over the natural resources associated with Federal lands.

Resources Addressed

In the process of studying the natural resources, the task force classified the natural resources into categories. These categories were established for purposes of analyzing the resources. The natural resources and/or categories of resources that the task force addressed in this project are presented below with a brief description for each. They are:

Timber
  Timber is harvested from Federal lands on a sustained-yield basis through carefully managed reforestation programs. The private contractor who is selected to harvest the timber only purchases the timber designated for harvest, while the ownership of the land remains with the Federal Government. The contractor is responsible for the actual removal of the timber from the public land area. Actual harvesting may take up to two or three years after areas have been "marked for cut."

Outer Continental Shelf Oil & Gas
  States have been granted the rights to natural resources within 3 nautical miles of their coastline, except for the Gulf of Mexico coasts of Texas and Florida, where State jurisdiction extends for 3 marine leagues. The Federal jurisdiction begins after the State jurisdiction ends and extends for at least 200 nautical miles seaward of the coastline. The Outer Continental Shelf (OCS) consists of over 1.4 billion acres of submerged lands seaward of State jurisdiction. The Federal Government manages the rights to oil, gas, and other minerals on the OCS. The Government issues leases that convey an exclusive right to explore for and develop oil and gas on the OCS, and maintain a royalty interest in any production saved, removed, or sold from a lease. Over 27 million acres of the OCS are currently under active lease. The OCS accounts for over 27% of the natural gas and 20% of the oil produced in the United States.

Leasable Minerals
  Leasable minerals include solid minerals (e.g., coal, oil shales, asphalt, phosphate, potash, sodium) and fluid minerals (e.g., onshore oil & gas, geothermal energy). The Federal Government is responsible for managing the mineral estate owned by the Federal Government that underlies approximately 564 million acres of surface land it owns. In addition, the government holds the mineral rights on split-estate lands for which the surface has been conveyed. The government allows these

minerals to be developed through leases. Lessees pay rental per acre to hold the leases and compensate the government for minerals removed with a royalty on the sales value.

Locatable Minerals

The class of economic minerals known as "locatable" minerals makes up a significant portion of the "economic" minerals. The class includes precious metals (e.g., gold and silver), ferrous metals, light metals, base metals, precious and semi-precious gemstones and a vast array of industrial minerals.

U.S. citizens and incorporated businesses are permitted to prospect for locatable minerals on Federal lands in nineteen states as long as those lands have not been closed or withdrawn from mining. If valuable mineral deposits are discovered, prospectors can file a claim giving them the right to use the land for mining-related activities and the right to sell the minerals extracted without paying a royalty to the Federal Government. A claimant desiring to obtain fee simple title to the land and the mineral rights can patent the claim for $2.50 or $5.00 an acre, depending on the type of claim. After the patent has been granted, the claim becomes private property.

Also, because mining operators are not required to report their production (extracted amount) from Federal lands and because the Federal Government is not required to collect such information, reliable figures may not be available to determine the total value of locatable minerals extracted from Federal lands.

Mineral Materials

Mineral materials include various common minerals, such as sand, gravel, and stones, which are considered part of the mineral estate owned by the Federal Government. The Federal Government manages these minerals on public lands and other lands under the jurisdiction of the government. Disposal of mineral materials is realized through sale contracts to private users or free use permits to states, counties, or other government entities for public projects. Also, a limited amount of mineral materials may be provided free to non-profit groups.

Grazing Uses

The United States owns public rangelands. Agencies of the United States Government are responsible for management of the natural resources on the surface of the lands for which stewardship has been entrusted to them. Federal agencies manage approximately 255,000,000 acres of grazing lands for domestic livestock use through 10-year permits or leases. In addition, 16 Alaska native corporations who own reindeer graze 5,000,000 acres without charge. The Federal Government does not transfer ownership or control of the rangelands because these public lands, by law, are held for multiple use.

Electromagnetic Spectrum

All sovereign nations own the rights to the electromagnetic spectrum within their boundaries. The U.S. Federal Government assigns the right to use portions of the spectrum to state and local governments and to the private sector for specific purposes. However, the Federal Government does not transfer ownership of the spectrum itself. A significant portion of the spectrum is reserved for defense and other government uses.

Nontraditional Resources

   The term "nontraditional resources" is used in this document to categorize other natural resources that are not addressed in any of the other categories of natural resources presented above, but for which a commercial market exits. The principal limitation of reporting information about nontraditional resources individually is the lack of data on them.

   The majority of nontraditional resources are non-timber vegetative products that are sold from public lands; however, there are others. Examples of nontraditional resources include Christmas trees and Christmas wreath materials, mushrooms, wild berries, medicinal herbs, cactus, and pine nuts. Through the Federal Government's forest management programs, the rights to remove non-timber vegetative products from public lands are conveyed upon payment of a permit fee to harvest them.

   Though many people may question the value of these resources and the amount of revenue they generate, there has been a dramatic increase in public interest and the market for these resources over the past few years. For example, in 1995, less than 1 million pounds of matsutake mushrooms were harvested from national forests, but 1.2 million pounds were harvested during an eight-week period in 1997.

   The natural resources identified and briefly described above are individually addressed in the **Reporting by Individual Resources** (Appendix A) of this paper.

Water Rights

 Water is a resource that is managed by the states. Each state has its own organization to administer water rights. Interstate water rights are administered by the states, using: 1) an agreement between states which indicates states' rights to use the water, 2) adjudication by the Supreme Court, or 3) Congressional decision. States administer water rights for Federal lands within a state. Federal action can pre-empt this, however, for various reasons, for example: 1) navigability of the water, 2) Federal environmental laws, and 3) Federal hydroelectric dams. However, because water rights are managed by the states, the Federal Government is rarely the owner of water rights and it rarely sells them. As a result, it does not have stewardship responsibility over water rights. Therefore, water rights were ultimately determined to be outside the scope of the natural resource project.

II. Objectives of Natural Resources Reporting

Background

The objectives outlined in Statement of Federal Financial Accounting Concept Statement (SFFAC) No. 1, *Objectives of Federal Financial Reporting*, continue to provide the framework for all projects addressed by the FASAB. In developing objectives for natural resources reporting, the task force used the basis of SFFAC No. 1 to ensure that all of the major objectives were considered for natural resources.

SFFAC No. 1 defines the four major objectives for Federal financial reporting:

Budgetary Integrity:

    Federal financial reporting should assist in fulfilling the government's duty to be publicly accountable for monies raised through taxes and other means and for their expenditure in accordance with the appropriations laws that establish the government's budget for a particular fiscal year and related laws and regulations.

Operating Performance:

    Federal financial reporting should assist report users in evaluating the service efforts, costs, and accomplishments of the reporting entity; the manner in which these efforts and accomplishments have been financed; and the management of the entity's assets and liabilities.

Stewardship:

    Federal financial reporting should assist report users in assessing the impact on the country of the government's operations and investments for the period and how, as a result, the government's and the nation's financial conditions have changed and may change in the future.

Systems and Control:

    Federal financial reporting should assist report users in understanding whether financial management systems and internal accounting and administrative controls are adequate to ensure that
- transactions are executed in accordance with budgetary and financial laws and other requirements, are consistent with the purposes authorized, and are recorded in accordance with Federal accounting standards;
- assets are properly safeguarded to deter fraud, waste, and abuse; and
- performance measurement information is adequately supported.

Based on the above objectives and discussions by the task force, the following major objectives were identified for natural resources reporting. The objectives are presented as those that relate to past performances and those that relate to future management. Reporting on our national wealth is also addressed.

Reporting on Past Performance

Natural resource reporting can report on past performance from a budgetary, operating, or stewardship perspective.

Budgetary integrity:
> Financial reporting on natural resources can provide information for decision makers and the public that will be useful in determining whether the entity has complied with laws governing the use of revenues received related to natural resources.

Operating performance:
> Financial reporting on natural resources can provide information for decision makers and the public that will be useful in evaluating the reporting entity's costs, accomplishments, and management of its assets and liabilities.

Stewardship:
> Financial reporting on natural resources can provide information for decision makers and the public that will be useful in assessing the entity's stewardship of its assets, including whether and to what extent benefits and burdens are passed from present to future taxpayers.

Information that would help meet these objectives include:

- government receipts (revenue) and offsetting collections reported according to their source,
- information about the extent of compliance with the budget and laws (e.g. compliance with any restrictions on the use/distribution of sales revenues).
- the net costs of operating natural resources programs compared with revenues generated,
- the amount (expressed in terms of market value [if available] or physical units) and condition/availability of the entity's natural resources,
- information pertaining to the resources currently leased, licensed for use by others, or otherwise conveyed to others for their use (but not sold),
- annual changes in the amount and condition of the natural resources,
- liabilities arising from the operation of natural resources programs and plans for their liquidation,
- extraction/production/consumption information.
- the value (if available) foregone or the amount of resources restricted by law or administratively and a description of their alternative use (e.g. timber restricted from sale because it is in national parks).

Reporting to Support Future Management

Natural resource reporting could also serve natural resources accounting by providing information relevant to policy decisions about the future management and the disposition of Federal natural resources. Many of the types of natural resource information that might be reported in financial statements are relevant to key policy issues about stewardship and natural resources management. Such policy issues include the following questions:

- What new authorities should be enacted to sell natural resources?

- Under what conditions should commercially valuable natural resources be withdrawn from availability for sale?

- For resources available for sale, when should they be offered and in what amounts?

- What policy or standard should govern the amounts the Government is to receive in return for the resources it sells?

Consideration of such questions by policy makers in the Congress and the Executive Branch and by the interested public may focus on specific resources in specific geographic areas or on policies for managing resources in the future.

Although it may seem that financial reporting could structure relevant information in a manner that facilitates these considerations, there are several important limitations that need to be recognized:

- financial reporting, particularly on balance sheets and the statement of net cost, requires an accuracy that usually does not exist for resources far in advance of their sale;

- financial reporting provides information in the aggregate for an agency, whereas much policy discussion focuses on specific resources in specific areas;

- financial reporting does a better job at organizing information about past transactions than about prospective transactions.

The task force gave careful consideration to the possibilities for providing information of the sort that would facilitate such policy discussions in financial reports in light of these limitations.

Reporting on the National Wealth in our Natural Resources

The possibility has been suggested that Federal accounting practices could assist in providing information on the status of the national wealth that is embodied in our endowments of natural resources. As part of its efforts, the task force received briefings on natural resource information from resource agencies such as the US Geological Survey and the Bureau of Land Management; and from the Bureau of Economic Analysis on the status of efforts to develop Environmental Satellite Accounts to the National Accounts that would display non-renewable resources.[1] The task force also had the benefit of work done by the World Resources Institute on accounting for natural resources in Indonesia and Costa Rica.[2]

The task force concluded, based on its review of this information, that the financial statements of Federal agencies may not be the best way to display information on the natural resource assets of the nation. Several factors support this conclusion. First, although the Federal Government owns significant natural resources, there is no resource category for which the Federal Government is the sole owner of all the resources. Thus, a full accounting for the nation's natural resources could not be produced with information limited to Federally owned resources.

Second, the natural resources owned by the Federal Government have several characteristics that make it difficult to provide a full accounting for them as assets. Most important is the fact that large amounts of natural resources currently have little or no commercial value despite the fact that they may have value at some time in the future. A good example of such a resource is coal (see Figure 2.1). The processes by which some parcels of resources gain sufficient value to be regarded as assets are only partly under the control of the agencies that manage the resources. Most of the processes that can make these resources valuable occur within the context of the markets for the resources and the products to which they contribute. The Federal and State agencies that regulate firms in these markets also have strong effects in determining what parcels of resource become valuable. In addition, in some cases, the benefit to the country through other uses of the land, such as, national parks or wilderness areas, are considered more valuable than commercial development.

Third, the current activities of Federal agencies do not produce comprehensive information about the value of the natural resources owned by the Federal Government. Information on the value of specific portions of Federal natural resource assets is produced as part of the management processes that lead to the sale of those resources; much less is known about the value of resources not being prepared for sale. Ironically, this means that Federal agencies know the most about the value and extent of natural resources parcels just at the time when they leave Federal ownership.

It may be more appropriate to develop an accounting for the nation's natural resource wealth through efforts such as those begun by the Bureau of Economic Analysis or the Interagency Working Group on

---

[1] See for example, Survey of Current Business, April 1994, U.S. Department of Commerce

[2] Repetto, Robert Accounts Overdue: Natural Resource Depreciation in Costa Rica, World Resources Institute, 1991. and Repetto, Robert, Wasting Assets: Natural Resources in National Income Accounts, World Resources Institute, 1989.

Sustainable Development Indicators which reports to the Council on Environmental Quality.

Figure 2.1
Example of Coal Resources

The Federal Government is the owner of a very substantial amount of coal resources, located primarily in western states. Of the 1.6 trillion tons of identified coal resources in the U.S., almost 1 trillion tons are in eight western states where about 60% are Federally owned. Because of the "checkerboard" land ownership patterns in the West, most coal mines in the West must combine reserves owned by Federal, State, private and Indian entities. Parcels of Federal coal become commercially valuable when there is a possibility of combining them into a mine with other nearby parcels.

Coal production in 1996 was about 1 billion tons. Assuming that mines generally have sufficient reserves to continue production from 20 to 50 years, only 20 to 50 billion tons of the 1.6 trillion tons are currently associated with operating mines. Of the remaining 1.55 trillion tons, only a small part will become commercially valuable over the next decade or two as new mines are needed to replace mines that have exhausted their reserves. Which parcels will become valuable at what time and at what values depend on variables such as regulation of emissions from coal burning, deregulation of the electric utility industry, and transportation costs.

It is clear from this example, that only a small portion of the Federal Government's coal resources could now be regarded as an asset for purposes of financial reporting. Parcels of Federal coal may become valuable only a matter of years before they are leased by the Department of the Interior. Estimates of their value become available months before leases are sold. These characteristics of coal resources and the processes through which they are managed lead the task force to the conclusion that information about quantities rather than dollar values would be most useful for financial reporting.

III. Context for Analysis -- Framework

Background

To properly address the area of accounting for natural resources, the task force needed a framework for understanding how natural resources are managed. Early in its work the task force recognized that natural resources managed by the Federal Government pass through a series of stages resulting from the sequence of management processes, i.e., decisions and transactions established under the Federal statutes that govern each resource. It was important for the task force to understand these stages, the nature of the information available about the quantity and value of resources at each stage, and the nature of the decisions and transactions that separate one stage from the next in the development of its recommendations.

Figure 3.1 shows a matrix of Federal natural resources stages, which identifies the categories of stocks and flows that are associated with the resources. This matrix was an analytical tool used by the task force to develop a common approach for understanding the various Federal natural resources management processes. The matrix presents the stages and flows closest to producing cash values first and those farthest from producing cash last.

For the most part, natural resources yield value to the Federal Government when the resources are sold or otherwise transferred from the government to the private sector. In some cases, the actual receipt of revenues occurs over a period of time in a manner that is specified to a permit, contract or lease. Further discussions relating to the stages and the stocks and flows of natural resources are presented in the following paragraphs.

Stages

The stages reflect decisions to make resources available for sale or change the status of the resource. The sequence of stages differs somewhat for different types of resources, because of differences in the processes used to manage the type of resource. It should be noted that a specific resource in a specific location may remain in a particular stage indefinitely, or for an extended period of time. The discussion below generally follows the chronological order of natural resources' management processes.

Although our natural resources matrix (see Figure 3.1 on page 16) recognizes an "undiscovered resources" stage, the natural resources management process sequence begins with the basic decision about whether or not the resource will be available for transfer to the private sector. It ends with the actual conveyance of ownership of the resource to a private entity. Once resources have been conveyed to the private sector, they are no longer under Federal management. However, several conveyance transactions require some type of continued Federal intervention. For example, the Bureau of Land Management is responsible for managing on-shore leasing and lease operations and the

Minerals Management Service is responsible for off-shore leasing and lease operations, as well as for collecting and distributing mineral revenues for both on-shore and off-shore minerals. The following stages are typical of Federal natural resources management:

Undiscovered Resources

Undiscovered resources are those resources postulated from geological information and theory to exist outside of known deposits.

Resources Not Available for Transfer

There are two conditions under which resources are not available for transfer. One is because the resources are legislatively withdrawn and the other is because the resources are administratively withdrawn. The two conditions are discussed below.

• Legislatively Withdrawn Resources -- those resources that by law can not be offered for transfer to private entities. Usually the resources are designated by geographical area. Examples include:
   - Oil and gas in areas of the OCS under Congressional leasing moratoria.
   - Timber and mineral resources in Wilderness Areas, National Parks, and Recreation Areas.
   - Oil and gas in the Arctic National Wildlife Refuge.
   - Coal resources in alluvial areas.
   - Locatable minerals in wilderness areas.

• Administratively Withdrawn Resources -- those resources in areas which by law could be offered for transfer to private entities, but which have been administratively withdrawn. Such resources could be made available for future transfer by administrative decision without change in law. Examples include:

   - Oil and gas resources in areas of the OCS not included in an approved 5-Year Leasing Program.
   - Resources in Marine Sanctuaries that cannot be extracted or used under the conditions of the sanctuary designation.
   - Resources in National Monuments that cannot be extracted or used under the conditions of the monument designation or management plan.
   - Timber resources in conservation areas.
   - Locatable minerals in scenic or recreational areas.

Resources Available for Transfer

There are three conditions under which resources are available for transfer. The three conditions are discussed below.

• Resources Planned to be Offered -- those resources for which it has been determined that specific types of resources in specific locations or within specific areas will be made available for transfer to private entities. Examples include:

- Oil and gas resources in areas selected for lease sales.
- Timber in areas to be included in planned timber sales.
- Areas open to claims under the Mining Law of 1872.

• Resources Under Contract but Not Conveyed -- those resources for which a prior transaction or process has resulted in a contract or other legal obligation under which Federal natural resources of a particular type and at a particular location will be conveyed to a private entity at some future time. Resources in this stage are still owned by the Federal Government and are expected to yield future revenues. Examples of resources under contract but not conveyed include:

- Oil and gas resources in tracts currently under lease under the OCS Lands Act.
- Timber in timber sale areas for which contracts have been sold.
- Locatable minerals in areas for which claims have been filed under the Mining Law of 1872.

• Other Available Resources -- those resources which are neither restricted by law nor administratively withdrawn, are outside of areas for which there are contracts to convey a resource, and are outside of areas for which the determination has been made to offer the resource for sale. Examples include:

- Unleased oil and gas resources in OCS planning areas in an approved 5 Year leasing program, but outside of areas in proposed lease sales.

Conveyed

Conveyance occurs when the ownership of the resource actually transfers from the government to a private entity. In many cases, a contract, lease or permit is sold or issued through an earlier transaction or transfer process. In some cases a consideration is paid at the time of this transaction as well as at the time the resource is conveyed to the private entity. In other cases, payment is made only when the resource is conveyed. In a few cases, the conveyance occurs without a prior contract.

Stocks and Flows

The stages identified above can be thought of in relationship to stocks and flows of resources. Whenever a decision is made or a transfer occurs, a flow results, which reduces the stock of the resource in one stage and increases the stock of the resource in another stage. In some cases a financial transaction and flow accompany the flow of resources from one stage to another. The final flow is the conveyance of the resource from Federal to private ownership.

At each stage, it is possible in principle to measure natural resource assets in both physical and financial terms. In practice, however, there are uncertainties about one or both types of measures, particularly in the early stages of management. Obviously, the greatest certainty occurs at the point in time when the resource is extracted and marketed. At this point, both the physical and financial measures of the resource are well known. Prior to that point, there are uncertainties that affect the ability to value a resource. Note that the conveyance of natural resources to the private sector is the primary flow associated with cash transactions.

Figure 3.1
Natural Resources Stages

STAGE	STOCKS		FLOWS					
			Increases & Decreases Due to Transfers (Government actions and transactions)		Other Increases & Decreases *		Extraction & Use	
	Physical	Financial	Physical	Financial	Physical	Financial	Physical	Financial
Conveyed	Not applicable							
Available							Not Applicable	
Under contract but not conveyed								
Planned to be offered							Not Applicable	
Other Available								
Not Available								
Administrative Withdrawal								
Legislative Withdrawal								
Undiscovered Resources								

* Changes in estimated amounts or financial value of the resources due to technological developments, improved information, natural processes or market processes.

IV. General Reporting Principles

Background

In the process of developing the general reporting principles, the task force was faced with three major issues or questions. They were:

- Should a value be reported for natural resources? If so, at what point in time should a value for natural resources be reported? Should this reporting occur in the principal financial statements or elsewhere, such as, an accountability report?

- How should the revenue generated from the sale of natural resources be accounted for and reported?

- How should the costs associated with the ownership and sale of natural resources be accounted for and reported?

In general, the task force concluded that the primary mechanism for reporting information about the natural resource assets under an agency's management should be stewardship reporting. Stewardship reporting would allow an agency to report meaningful and complete information about natural resources for sale, as well as resources that are not available for sale (e.g., due to legislative and administrative withdrawals.)

The task force concluded that valuation of assets for purposes of Balance Sheet presentation would require assurance of the intended commercial use of the asset. Where the Federal Government is not assured that the asset will be used for commercial purposes, there is no basis for determination of the commercial value. Therefore, until a natural resource is placed on the commercial market (i.e., offered for sale) and the value is know (i.e., an actual offer is received), assurance cannot be made that the asset will be sold for commercial use.

The task force did, however, determine that the Federal Government has the responsibility to report natural resources that may be sold for commercial use and other data related to natural resources for which the Federal Government has stewardship responsibility. The task force believes that stewardship reporting would be the most effective way to discharge this reporting responsibility.

The task force did not reach a consensus on how revenue generated from the sale of natural resources should be recognized. The following two options discussed by the task force are provided in more detail later in this chapter for your consideration.

- Reporting all natural resource revenues on the Statement of Custodial Activities and

• Reporting all natural resource revenues on the Statement of Net Costs.

In relation to costs associated with the ownership and sale of natural resources, the task force reached specific conclusions on each type of cost. These conclusions are in accordance with SFFAS No. 4, *Managerial Cost Accounting Concepts and Standards for the Federal Government*.

Detailed discussions are provided on the pages to follow on:

• reporting information about natural resource assets,
• accounting and reporting revenues,
• accounting and reporting for costs, and
• prices set by law or regulators.

Appendix A, **Reporting by Individual Resource**, discusses the current accounting treatment and issues for each type of natural resource addressed by the task force.

Reporting Information about Natural Resource Assets

Within the existing scope of Federal accounting and reporting, there are multiple options for reporting information about natural resources owned by the Federal Government. Different options may be possible for a given natural resource according to the "stage" of the natural resource identified (i.e., undiscovered resources, not available for transfer, available for transfer, conveyed). Separate reporting options might also be chosen for various natural resources due to differences in the terms of sale or the attributes of natural resources. In addition, multiple options may be chosen for a single category of a resource (e.g. resources identified for sale might be both recognized and discussed in a footnote).

As illustrated in the Chart below, the options available to an entity for reporting information about natural resources include recognition of an asset in the accounting records of an agency, footnote disclosure, other reporting vehicles, and even silence (i.e., no reporting at all.) Each of these reporting options has specific advantages and disadvantages. A description of each reporting option follows the Chart.

Reporting					
Recognition	**Disclosure**	**Other Reporting**			**No Reporting**
Principal Financial Statements	Footnotes	Stewardship Reporting	MD&A (Overview)	Other Reported Information	Silence

• Recognition -- Reporting of information in the principal financial statement when an accounting entry with a specific dollar amount is posted to an account in the entity's general ledger. The principal financial statements of the entity represent a summary of all of the general ledger accounts of the entity at a point in time. Recognition is only possible when the transaction is measurable in dollars and the amount can be reasonably estimated.

• Disclosure -- Disclosure refers to the reporting of information in the notes (footnotes) to principal financial statements. This information should be concise and either provides additional information about transactions recognized in the principal financial statements or explains why certain data or transactions may have been excluded from recognition. Footnote disclosure is regarded as an integral part of the basic financial statements.

• Other Reporting -- A reporting option used in this document to identify other mechanisms of reporting information about natural resources, in lieu of the principal financial statements. Included are:

> - Stewardship Reporting -- Additional reporting used to provide more extensive information that is critical to understanding a reporting entity's financial condition, but which cannot be measured in purely financial terms and which cannot be adequately addressed by concise footnotes.

> - Management's Discussion and Analysis -- Additional reporting used to provide a clear and concise description of the reporting entity and its mission; activities, program, and financial results; and financial position.

> - Other Reported Information -- Other reporting mechanisms used to report relevant information not reported in any of the previously identified reporting options. Examples include required supplementary information (RSI) and other accounting information (OAI).

• No Reporting -- There are instances where nothing will be reported about some types of natural resources. These would include natural resources not included in the scope of this project (e.g., air, stock of game, fisheries, and wildlife habitat). This may be because the information about the natural resource is insignificant, immaterial, or too speculative, or because the natural resource is beyond the scope of required reporting. However, as conditions and/or information about these types of natural resources change, the reporting requirements for them can be revisited.

General Discussion

After reviewing all of the alternatives for reporting information about natural resources and the reporting requirements or principles for each, the task force determined that three options would be most likely to satisfy the natural resources reporting objectives. The three options considered and examined in detail were Recognition, Disclosure, and Stewardship Reporting. The task force believed that the other available reporting options--MD&A and other reported information--were not mechanisms intended to provide the amount of detail and/or focus on specific information that could be provided by recognition, disclosure, or stewardship reporting. For each of the three reporting options that was determined to be most likely to satisfy the natural resources reporting objectives, the paragraphs below contain a general discussion, an analysis of reporting alternatives, a suggested reporting principle, and the advantages and disadvantages of the suggested principle. Although the task force found it necessary to reach a conclusion in each area, it is aware that the Board, during its own deliberations, may not reach the same conclusion.

1.   <u>Recognition</u>

      Various Statements of Federal Financial Accounting Standards provide a definition for assets. The definition states that assets are tangible or intangible items owned by the Federal Government that would have probable economic benefits that can be obtained or controlled by a Federal Government entity. The term recognition (or recognize), as used in Statements of Federal Financial Accounting Standards, means the process of formally recording or incorporating an item into entity accounts to be reported in the financial statements as an asset, liability, revenue, expense, or the like. In theory, recognition is only possible when the transaction recording an item is measurable in dollars and the amount can be reasonably estimated.

Analysis of Recognition Alternative

Presented below are various points in time that were considered for recognizing a natural resource on the Balance Sheet. The points in time that were considered are:

- when discovered,
- at certain points prior to sale, and
- at time of sale.

a. Recognition when Discovered - The task force discussed Balance Sheet recognition of natural resource assets extensively. One of the alternatives considered was to recognize natural resources on the Balance Sheet as assets when their existence became known. However, briefings provided by various resource experts impressed upon the task force that the difficulty in reasonably estimating the quantity and value of natural resources impacts the ability to recognize these resources on the Balance Sheet. If these estimates were recognized, they may be likely to distort the Statement of Net Cost, as discussed more fully below. Thus, while natural resources should be properly recognized when they fall under existing standards, (e.g. the acquisition of helium for future sale is covered by SFFAS #3), they should also, as a general rule, be reported as stewardship information to provide a complete picture of natural resource activity and status.

b. Recognition at Certain Points Prior to Sale - The task force considered recognizing some natural resource assets when it becomes possible to estimate quantities to be offered for sale and the related market price. For example, there are two possible points when enough information is available prior to sale when the financial value of certain resources (e.g., timber and mineral materials resources) might be reasonably estimable. Specifically, these points are when:

- the natural resource is identified as "planned to be offered" -- At this point, the agency has determined that specific types of resources in specific locations will be made available for sale.

- the natural resource is under contract but not conveyed -- At this point, the quantity to be sold is reasonably certain, however the market price may fluctuate depending on when the resource is actually extracted or harvested. For example, timber is often placed under contract for sale months or years in advance of the actual cutting (and "conveyance") of the timber.

In both of these cases, the estimated value would be based on the potential sale price of the asset. However, in reviewing these options, the task force considered the impact that Balance

Sheet recognition of the sales value of a resource would have on the Statement of Net Cost. For example, if a resource is capitalized based on its future sale value, and the entity incurs any costs associated with the sale, the Statement of Net Cost would reflect a "loss" to the government on that transaction, regardless of whether the government conducted that transaction efficiently. Thus, this approach would misstate the value of the natural resource as recorded on the Balance Sheet by at least the amount of the sale costs.

In addition, while considering this alternative, the task force also considered "discounting" the sale value in some way, but found no reliable method to accomplish this. Specifically, the task force noted:

- Valuation of a natural resource based on discounted sales value would require numerous assumptions and estimates, making the range of possible values large and subject to wide fluctuations; and
- The use of an estimated asset value could cause distortions in the "Cost of Sales" and the "Net Cost of Operations" line items on the Statement of Net Cost.

c.   Recognition At Time of Sale - The closer you get to the selling point, the better the estimate you can make as to how much you will get for the sale of a resource. As noted above, for most resources, the quantity and market value cannot be reasonably estimated prior to the point at which the asset is sold. Therefore, there is no relevance in recognizing the asset on the Balance Sheet at the time of sale.

<u>Suggested Reporting Principle</u>

Although the task force believes that the value of natural resources available for sale is important information that should be available to the user of financial statements, it was concluded that Balance Sheet recognition is not the most effective or reliable method of communicating this information. Rather, this information should be reported in the Notes to the Financial Statements and as stewardship information. Further, for entities with significant natural resources, a line with no dollar amount could be placed on the Balance Sheet to direct readers to the footnote reference. If a resource sale results in a large net profit in a given year, this should be explained in a footnote to include information about prices and quantities sold.

Advantages:

- Reporting is reliable and large fluctuations are minimized.
- Reporting is clear and not misleading.
- Management's discretion on the reported amounts is minimized.
- Reported amounts are accurate and verifiable.

Disadvantages:

- There is no recognition of assets available for sale.
- No reporting is provided on the face of the financial statements, although full reporting is obtained through the footnotes and stewardship reporting.

2.   Disclosure

Disclosure refers to the reporting of information in the notes (footnotes) to principal financial statements. Footnotes traditionally include information necessary to understand the amounts presented on the principal financial statements, as well as information about any items that would be included in the financial statements if quantifiable financial information about the item where available.

Analysis of Disclosure Alternatives

Footnote disclosure is intended to enable the financial statement user to better interpret and assess the information contained in the financial statements. Generally, information presented in the footnotes tends to be precise, objective, verifiable, and historical. Information in the footnotes may include items such as:

- Qualitative information about items recognized in the financial statements.
- Quantitative information about items recognized in the financial statements.
- Information about items not recognized in the financial statements.

Suggested Reporting Principle

The footnotes could be used to convey information necessary for understanding natural resources. Footnote disclosures are intended to specifically include information about what has been presented on the face of financial statements as well as what has been excluded. In addition, footnotes could be used to refer the reader to stewardship reporting for more complete information.

Advantages:

- Disclosures are complete and informative.
- A clear link between Balance Sheet and stewardship reporting is provided.

Disadvantages:

- Information may appear in two locations (i.e., footnotes and stewardship reporting), with some duplication of information.

3.   Stewardship Reporting

Stewardship reporting is used to present discussion, charts, graphs and other financial and nonfinancial information necessary for the reader's understanding of the resources entrusted the Federal Government and the reporting entity.

Analysis of Stewardship Reporting Alternatives

Stewardship reporting is a fairly new reporting vehicle, and the content of this type of reporting is still under development. However, stewardship reporting would generally be lengthier and include more analysis, interpretation, and discussion than the footnotes. Stewardship reporting would include information to highlight the long-term nature of natural resources and to demonstrate accountability over the items reported.

The Stewardship information may include any or all of the information listed below.

- Information on resources available for sale, including:

  -- Estimated quantity of the resource available for sale
  -- Changes in quantity during the period in total and by status (e.g., available for sale, withdrawn, etc.)
  -- Existing plans for sale
  -- Method for determining prices, (e.g., market price or regulation)

- Information on limitations and restrictions on sale, including Legislative and Administrative Withdrawals (acres and discussion):

  -- Quantities related to administratively and legislatively withdrawn resources would be reported only when that information is available and relevant to current circumstances and decisions (e.g., mineral resources under existing national parks would not be estimated or disclosed).

- Deferred maintenance estimates and assessment of condition (e.g., rangeland used for grazing)

- Other relevant information and discussion

<u>Suggested Reporting Principle</u>

Stewardship reporting could be used as the primary tool for reporting natural resource information.   It is expected that stewardship reporting would provide a complete assessment of the natural resources of an agency, even if some of this information is also disclosed in the footnotes.

Advantages:

- Provides management with the flexibility necessary to ensure a complete assessment of natural resources.
- Provides the ability to display non-financial data, that may or may not be linked to financial data.
- Provides the ability to use graphics, charts, and other visual aids.
- Allows reporting even when management's knowledge is incomplete, for example when quantities or potential values are unknown.
- No single measure is necessary.
- Full reporting is provided even though a single measure of financial position does not exist.
- Data is provided within existing reporting framework.

Disadvantages:

- Data is not provided in a principal financial statement (therefore, the balance sheet may not provide a complete picture of financial position.)

Accounting and Reporting for Revenue

General Discussion

Revenue is an inflow of resources that the government demands, earns, or receives by donation. Revenue arises from exchange transactions and nonexchange transactions[3]. Exchange revenue is an inflow of resources to a government entity that the entity has earned. It arises from exchange transactions in which each party to the transaction sacrifices value and receives value in return. Such revenue should be recognized at established prices when services are performed or rendered or when goods from inventory are delivered. The following two paragraphs from SFFAS 7 outline the recognition of exchange revenue.

> Exchange revenue should be recognized in determining the net cost of operations of the reporting entity during the period. The exchange revenue should be recognized regardless of whether the entity retains the revenue for its own use or transfers it to other entities. Gross and net cost should be calculated as appropriate to determine the costs of outputs and the total net cost of operations of the reporting entity. The components of the net cost calculation should separately include the gross cost of providing goods or services that earned exchange revenue, less the exchange revenue earned, and the resulting difference. The components of net cost should also include separately the gross cost of providing goods, services, benefit payments, or grants that did not earn exchange revenue.

> The net amount of gains (or losses) should be subtracted from (or added to) gross cost to determine net cost in the same manner as exchange revenue is subtracted. Exchange revenue that is immaterial or cannot be associated with particular outputs should be deducted separately in calculating the net cost of the program, suborganization, or reporting entity as a whole as appropriate. Nonexchange revenues and other financing sources should not be deducted from the gross cost in determining the net cost of operations for the reporting entity.[4]

All sales of natural resources or the rights to use natural resources are exchange revenues of the Federal Government. The government may sell:

• the resource itself (e.g., timber, extracted oil and gas),

---

[3] Nonexchange revenues arise primarily from exercise of the government's power to demand payment form the public (e.g., taxes, duties, fines, and penalties), but also include donations. Nonexchange revenue should be recognized when a specifically identifiable, legally enforceable claim to resources arises, to the extent that collection is probable and the amount is measurable.

[4] SFFAS 7, paragraphs 43 & 44.

- the right to search for the resource in a specific location for a specific period of time (e.g. a mineral lease), in this case, the resource itself is not sold until extracted,
- the right to use the resource for a period of time, with ownership of the resource remaining with the government at all times (e.g. electromagnetic spectrum, land for grazing), or
- the land containing the resource, irrespective of the presence or absence of natural resources (e.g. 1872 mining law).

During the task force discussions, the issue of natural resource revenue recognition was heavily debated. The discussions were primarily focused on the fact that SFFAS No. 7, *Accounting for Revenue and Other Financing Sources and Concepts for Reconciling Budgetary and Financial Accounting*, provides an exception for entities, such as the rents and royalties collected by the Minerals Management Service (MMS) on the Outer Continental Shelf, that recognize "virtually no costs" (either during the current period or during past periods) in connection with earning revenue that it collects.

SFFAS 7 states that:

> The collecting entity should not offset its gross costs by such exchange revenue in determining its net cost of operations. If such exchange revenue is retained by the entity, it should be recognized as a financing source in determining the entity's operating results. If, instead, such revenue is collected on behalf of other entities (including the U.S. Government as a whole), the entity that collects the revenue should account for that revenue as a custodial activity, i.e., an amount collected for others.

The following excerpts are from the SFFAS 7 Basis for Conclusions that explains the Board's reasoning for this revenue recognition exception.

> Matching revenue with cost in a uniform manner is essential in evaluating agency performance and setting price. Cost and revenue must pertain to the same output in order to estimate the extent to which the revenue covers the cost. Therefore, costs should be matched against the provision of goods and services with revenue matched against those costs and thus with revenue also matched against the same provision of goods and services. When this is done, the gross and net cost of an entity can be compared with the related outputs and outcomes to evaluate its operating performance, pricing policy, and economic decisions. Similarly, when this is done, the net cost to the taxpayer can be estimated for the entity's related outputs provided to the public. *(Par 118)*

> In exceptional cases, an entity may recognize virtually no costs in connection with earning exchange revenue that it collects. A major example for many years has been the Minerals Management Service (MMS) of the Department of the Interior. It manages energy and other mineral resources on the Outer Continental Shelf (OCS) and collects rents,

royalties, and bonuses due the Government and Indian tribes from minerals produced on the OCS and other Federal and Indian lands. The rents, royalties, and bonuses are exchange revenues, earned by sales in the market. If the value of natural resources were recognized as an asset by MMS, then depletion could be recognized as a cost according to the units of production method as minerals were extracted. The revenue from rents, royalties, and bonuses could then be matched against MMS's gross cost, including depletion and minor other costs, to determine its net cost of operations. *(Par 140)*

MMS does not recognize a depletion cost for various reasons, including the fact that under present accounting standards the value of natural resources is not recognized as an asset. As a result, this exchange revenue cannot be matched against the economic cost of operations and bears little relationship to the recognized cost of MMS. Therefore, it should not be subtracted from MMS's gross cost in determining its net cost of operations. If it were subtracted, the relationship between MMS's net cost of operations and its measures of performance would be distorted. The net cost of operations of the Department of the Interior would likewise be distorted. *(Par 141)*

Views similar to the above Basis for Conclusions on the recognition of some Federal natural resource revenues are also expressed in Appendix B of this document, *Minority Comments on General Reporting Principles*.

Based on its discussions, the task force did not reach a consensus on how revenue generated from natural resources should be reported. They did agree that the standards created for recognizing and reporting natural resource revenue should reflect consistent treatment so that any natural resource revenue that may be encountered by a Federal agency will be treated in a similar manner. Therefore, the task force provides, for consideration, two options that were proposed and discussed by members of the task force. The two options are as follows:

- reporting all natural resource revenues on the Statement of Custodial Activities and
- reporting all natural resource revenues on the Statement of Net Costs.

Each of the above options is further discussed in the following paragraphs.

Option 1: *Reporting All Natural Resource Revenues on the Statement of Custodial Activities*

As noted above, SFFAS No. 7 requires that entities such as the Minerals Management Service report the revenues collected as rents and royalties on the Outer Continental Shelf (OCS) as a custodial activity. These revenues are reported on the Statement of Custodial Activities because the entity "recognizes virtually no costs in connection with the revenue collected." Based on research by the task force, it was determined that many other natural resource revenues are reported on the Statement of Net Cost of Operations. The task force discussed the option of recognizing all natural resource revenues that are collected and are used to finance the Government as a whole or programs of other entities rather than their own activities, on the Custodial Statement.[5]

The Custodial Statement is designed to match collections for others against the disposition of collections, and the primary focus of the Statement is the tracking of non-exchange tax revenue. The Custodial Statement in its current format does not allow for the presentation of natural resource revenues matched against those costs associated with managing and selling the natural resource. Any attempt to match direct costs against revenues on this Statement would require significant changes to content and presentation of the Statement as well as the Statement of Net Cost if costs were removed from it.

However, the option to report all natural resource revenues on the Custodial Statement would allow for consistency in reporting natural resource revenues of the Federal Government. See **Attachment A** for the task force's suggested changes to SFFAS No. 7 that would specifically require all natural

---

[5] According to SFFAC No. 2, *Entity and Display:* A separate statement of custodial activities would be appropriate for those entities whose primary mission is collecting taxes or other revenues, particularly sovereign revenues that are intended to finance the entire Government's operations, or at least the programs of other entities, rather than their own activities. The revenues should be characterized by those agencies as custodial revenues. The statement should display the sources and amounts of the collections of custodial revenues, any increases or decreases in amounts collectable but not collected, the disposition of the collections through transfers to other entities, the amounts retained by the collecting entity, and any increase or decrease in the amounts to be transferred.

resource revenues to be reported as a custodial activity.

Option 2: *Reporting all natural resource revenues on the Statement of Net Costs.*

Revenue earned from the sale of natural resources is exchange revenue and costs are incurred by agencies to manage the assets and the programs that produce these revenues. The task force noted three elements of "cost of sales" to be considered when comparing the costs associated with a natural resource with the proceeds from the sale of that resource. All of these costs are reported on the Statement of Net Cost. The costs are:

- the cost of the natural resource to the government;
- the costs of managing the resource; and
- the costs of selling the resource.

In most cases, no direct, identifiable cost to the government is associated with acquisition of natural resources. There was some variability in the extent of natural resource management costs. However, those agencies that did incur management costs normally incurred those costs as part of the agency's overall stewardship responsibilities and would have incurred at least some portion of those costs even if no natural resources were sold. Cost of selling is normally incurred near the time of the earning of revenue, but these costs do not normally have a direct relationship to the revenue earned. Thus, on the whole, the revenue earned on the sale of any natural resource cannot be directly attributable to the costs associated with the acquisition, management, and selling of that resource. Rather, the revenue earned from the sale of any natural resources is generally dependent upon some combination of market value and regulatory requirements. For most Federal agencies, revenue generation is one of several goals of natural resource management, and general management costs cannot be directly assigned to natural resource sales. However, the revenue from the sale of natural resources is related to the agency operations and is related to the costs incurred in agency operations.

The natural resource asset itself may not have an acquisition cost that is comparable to its sale price. Many believe that presenting natural resource revenue on the Statement of Net Cost will distort this Statement. However, due to this lack of "acquisition costs," the reader should understand the nature of the sales transaction regardless of where the revenue is presented in the financial statements.

The natural resource revenues earned by various Federal agencies are fundamentally the same, that is, something of value is sold at a price. Currently, most natural resource revenues appear as revenue in the Statement of Net Costs of the agency that earns the revenue. However, according to SFFAS 7, under exceptional circumstances, such as oil and gas royalty and lease revenues collected by the Minerals Management Service, an entity that recognizes virtually no costs in connection with earning the revenue it collects should report that revenue on the Statement of Custodial Activity. All agencies incur some costs related to managing and selling the resource. However, the amount of identifiable cost that can be directly associated with the revenue stream may vary significantly according to the nature of the asset and the management goals of the agency. In some cases these costs are significant in comparison to revenue generated (e.g. USFS Timber sales), while in other cases the costs are minuscule (e.g. sale of pine nuts and other miscellaneous vegetative products by the Bureau of Land Management). However, there is no substantive difference in the nature of the different types of natural resource revenue (i.e., both oil and gas lease revenue is fundamentally the same as timber sales).

Since these exchange revenues are earned via agency operations, they should be reported on a statement that is linked with the other principal financial statements. Under current accounting standards, the assets, liabilities, and equity are reported on the Balance Sheet, and the flow accounts are reported in total on the Statement of Changes in Net Position. A portion of these flow accounts (expenses and exchange revenue) is presented in more detail on the Statement of Net Cost. Currently, the Statement of Net Cost is the reporting vehicle for exchange revenue, and the Statement of Custodial Activity is essentially a "memorandum" Statement that does not link directly with the other basic financial statements.

For example, the fiscal year 1997 government-wide consolidated financial statements disclose costs of $29.1 billion and revenue of $1.9 billion for "Natural Resources and Environment." These amounts do not include the $6 billion from the sale and lease of Outer Continental Shelf resources. The fact that natural resources provide a revenue stream to the Federal Government and partially offset the cost of managing those resources for the nation is not disclosed to the reader. Likewise, at the agency level, it is true that the Minerals Management Service spends approximately $250 million per year to manage resources and sales activity that result in an inflow to the Federal Government of several billion dollars. The public should be aware that this particular activity of the Federal Government results in a gain, in cash terms. Of course, the MMS report, as with all other reports disclosing significant natural resource revenue, would include disclosures about the fact that the resources sold do not have an "acquisition cost" and so the reported gain should be considered in relationship to the depletion of natural resource reserves.

Based on the above discussion, the task force developed an option to eliminate the exception in SFFAS 7, paragraph 45. The existing Statement of Net Cost of Operations would then accommodate all natural resource reporting, both at the entity level and the consolidated statement level.

As illustrated below, presentation changes on the Statement of Net Cost would involve adding a subtotal to clearly separate natural resource revenues from the cost of operations not directly related to the sale of natural resources. In this way:

- all exchange revenues would be presented on one statement;
- costs of selling directly attributable to the natural resources revenues could be matched with that revenue without removing these costs from the Statement of Net Costs ;
- revenues would be presented on the same statement as the costs incurred to manage the related assets, although not directly matched against those costs; and
- net costs associated with agency operations would continue to be clearly identifiable.

Sample Statement of Net Cost

Operation of Agency Programs	
Operating Expenses	XXXX
Revenues Related to Operations	XX
Net	XXXX
Other Gains and Losses	XX
Net Cost of Agency Operations	XXXX
Other Programs	
Direct Sales and Management Costs	XXXX
Less: Natural Resource Revenue	X
Net Results of Other Programs	XXXX
Net Results of Federal Programs	X

Accounting and Reporting for Costs

General Discussion

The concepts of managerial cost accounting, presented in SFFAS No. 4, *Managerial Cost Accounting Concepts and Standards for the Federal Government*, describe the relationship among cost accounting, financial reporting, and budgeting. The five standards presented in SFFAS No. 4 set forth the fundamental elements of managerial cost accounting: (1) accumulating and reporting costs of activities on a regular basis for management information purposes, (2) establishing responsibility segments to match costs with outputs, (3) determining full costs of government goods and services, (4) recognizing the costs of goods and services provided among Federal entities, and (5) using appropriate costing methodologies to accumulate and assign costs to outputs.

These standards are based on sound cost accounting concepts and are broad enough to allow maximum flexibility for agency managers to develop costing methods that are best suited to their operational environment. Also, the managerial cost accounting standards and practices will evolve and improve as agencies gain experience in using them.

Analysis of Accounting and Reporting for Costs Alternatives

Various types of cost were identified by the task force during its examination of costs associated with natural resources. The types of cost that were discussed were:

- Cost of Resources Sold
- Cost of Selling
- Cost of Management
- Transfer of Revenue/Distribution of Receipts

The cost, a suggested reporting principle, and advantages and disadvantages for the suggested reporting principle are presented in the following paragraphs for each type of cost.

1.   Cost of Resources Sold

The possible options for the recognition of "cost of resources sold" are dependent upon whether the natural resource has or has not been previously recognized as an asset. If an asset has been recognized on the Balance Sheet, that asset must be removed from the Balance Sheet at time of sale resulting in an expense on the Statement of Net Cost. If natural resources are not capitalized, there is no capital consumption type cost associated with the sale of natural resources. Presently, most natural resources are not capitalized by reporting entities on the Balance Sheet because of the difficulty in reasonably estimating the quantity and value of natural resources.

The agencies' lack of reliable measures of acquisition costs of natural resources can be attributed to one or more of the following reasons:

a. The natural resources were acquired as a result of the Federal government's sovereign powers, e.g., the radio spectrum.
b. Acquisition costs were fully expensed at time of purchase and historical records no longer exist and/or are not relevant for Balance Sheet valuation.
c. Agencies would have to utilize large amounts of resources to survey large tracts of land to estimate the value of natural resources that are costly to locate and whose values are uncertain.
d. There are no recent market transactions that provide an objective measure of the specific natural resource's value.

As a result the cost associated with a natural resource valuation cannot be determined with accounting precision.

Thus, the agencies' gross costs during a fiscal year would be their administrative costs, selling costs, and the market value of the rights to natural resources that generated exchange revenues during the same fiscal year. In effect, in cases where the rights to natural resources are sold for market value, the exchange revenue and the gross costs would increase by the same amount, and the net costs would only reflect the much smaller administrative and selling costs of the agency. However, this approach would be likely to cause substantial distortions in the Balance Sheet and the Statement of Net Costs to handle the treatment of the acquisition cost based on the changing market value of assets reported.

Consequently, most methods of imputing a "cost of goods sold" would, in one form or another, merely match the sales price against itself. To report reliable information, when comparing the inherent value of resources sold against the value received, will require reporting beyond the presentation of one simple number, which can best be done in a footnote or stewardship information.

Suggested Reporting Principle

The cost of resources sold should reflect the removal of previously recognized assets from the Balance Sheet, but should not be "imputed" when no such value exists.

Advantages:

- This approach would minimize manipulation of the Statement of Net Cost (since the imputed value of assets sold would be subject to numerous assumptions).
- Known information about the value of natural resources sold as compared to value received would be reported in the text of the footnotes and/or stewardship report.

Disadvantages:

- The Statement of Net Cost does not recognize the value of natural resources sold.

2.   Cost of Selling

The cost of selling consists of costs incurred for sale preparation and for activities that occur over the period of the sale of the natural resource. These costs include development of resource plans (e.g., 1 year, 5 year, 10 year) and environmental impact analysis prior to offering the resource for sale, and the costs of offering and awarding the resource sales. Currently, these costs are usually expensed in the period they are incurred. The alternative would be to capitalize and amortize these costs over the period that revenue is generated.

> **NOTE**: Prior to FY 1993, one reporting entity capitalized the costs associated with the sale of a particular natural resource and expensed the cost over the life of a sale contract. This methodology was developed by the reporting entity in conjunction with GAO as directed by the Congress. However, due to problems with a subsidiary system that was a feeder system for financial statement purposes, the entity's IG strongly advised the entity to discontinue using the subsidiary system as a feeder system. As a result, certain costs could no longer be capitalized and amortized over the life of a contract.

Suggested Reporting Principle

Accounting for the cost of selling natural resources should follow the general principles of SFFAS No. 4.

Advantages:

- Costs are matched with revenue.
- Costs of programs and the Net Cost are more complete and accurate.

Disadvantages:

- Since this approach may require change in reporting entities' accounting policies, it may take time to implement

3. Cost of Management

The cost of managing natural resources which will eventually be sold tend to be indistinguishable from the costs of managing other resources or carrying out legislatively mandated missions. For example, the land management activities of the Bureau of Land Management benefit both revenue producing and non-revenue producing lands.

In limited cases, such as timber management in areas designated for sale, it may be possible to separate management costs between those that benefit resources to be sold from those that benefit resources in general. On the other hand, the Bureau of Land Management manages its rangeland for multiple uses, including grazing, recreation and preservation, and any management activities performed would continue regardless of whether portions of the land are leased for grazing. In this case, no portion of this management cost should be allocated to "cost of goods sold".

However, in identifying costs to match against future revenue, management must bear in mind the extent to which those costs are incurred because of the agency's responsibility to manage the resources entrusted to it. Costs that are part of an agency's stewardship responsibility that are not intended to increase the flow of future revenue should not be matched against revenue. For most agencies, revenue production is a byproduct of natural resource management, and the Statement of Net Cost should clearly reflect the cost of the agency's primary mission (stewardship) rather than a secondary mission (revenue production). No costs should be capitalized and matched against revenue unless those costs were intended to enhance future revenue streams rather than to fulfill the agency's stewardship responsibility.

In accounting for the cost of managing natural resources, the choices include expensing the cost in the period or capitalizing the cost to match it against future sale.

Suggested Reporting Principle

Costs that are intended to enhance future revenue should be considered costs of selling as discussed in the previous section. Accounting for the costs of managing natural resources should follow the general principles of SFFAS No. 4.

Advantages:

- Program costs are complete, accurate and clearly report the agency's operating activity and primary mission.
- Costs incurred during the period are presented in that period and are not hidden as capitalized assets.

Disadvantages:

- Net revenue may be overstated if a portion of management costs improved the revenue flow.

4. <u>Transfer of Revenue/Distribution of Receipts</u>

In many cases, the agency that earns exchange revenue must transfer some or all of the proceeds to other Federal agencies. In addition, under law, many Federal agencies must share the proceeds of grazing, timber sales and other natural resource sales with state and local governments. This "sharing" of revenue represents an outflow of resources from the Federal Government as a whole. In these cases, the revenues are earned from assets that are owned by the Federal Government. The sharing occurs under legislation or other provisions, but is essentially a voluntary transfer to state and local governments by the part of the Federal Government.

In limited cases, the underlying assets are actually owned by the other party (e.g. Indian lands held in trust by the Federal Government). In these cases, the Federal Government has no revenue for the collections or expense for the transfer out, but merely acts as agent for the other party.

The treatment of the transfers, especially transfers outside the Federal Government, is a critical component in the analysis of government sales activity. There is an ongoing political debate over whether the government "loses money" on revenue transaction due to legislative requirements to transfer a portion of the proceeds to state and local governments.

As provided in SFFAS No.7, transfers between Federal agencies are currently recognized as "transfers" that have no impact on the Statement of Net Cost. Theoretically, transfers of Federal resources to state and local governments could be considered an expense of the Federal Government or a reduction in Federal revenue (e.g. contra revenue).

<u>Suggested Reporting Principle</u>

For revenue transferred to other Federal agencies, as provided by SFFAS No. 7, the collecting agency would recognize the transfer out on the Statement of Changes in Net Position. These transactions should be clearly identified and explained (in footnotes and/or the stewardship report) so that the reader understands the difference between the costs of goods sold and cost of selling associated with the revenue stream, and independent decisions to share a portion of proceeds with other governments.

Advantages:

- The full cost of government activities and decisions are clearly disclosed.

Disadvantages:

- The transfers of revenue and the distribution of receipts are not recognized as a program cost.

Prices Set by Law or Regulations

General Discussion

During our research in the area of natural resources of the Federal Government, we determined that there are situations where law or regulation (e.g., the Mining Law of 1872) sets the sale price of the resource rather than market forces. As a result of these laws and regulations, the value received for the sale of a natural resource is much less than the fair value of that resource.

Analysis of Options

The task force is aware that major difficulties exist in recognizing such information because of the difficulty in reliably measuring a transaction that did not occur. In addition, for resources such as forage where the government controls a substantial amount of the resource, the current "market price" does not necessarily reflect what the market price would be if government-owned resources were subject to market forces.

Suggested Reporting Principle

Footnote disclosure and other accompanying information should be used to report situations where prices are set by regulation rather than market forces, including a discussion of how prices are determined and differences between market rates and government rates, if available, as outlined in paragraphs 46 & 47 in SFFAS 7.

Advantages:

•   Management is given some flexibility to report what they can, based on the knowledge available, and fully explain the assumptions and limitations inherent in the information.
•   The information reported is not misleading

Disadvantages:

•   Amounts are not recognized in the financial statements.

Summary of Minority Comments on General Reporting Principles

Appendix B (*Minority Comments on General Reporting Principles*) raises three concerns related to the reporting options discussed in this section. First, Appendix B suggests that the basic concepts of SSFAS No. 7 are valid, and that sales of natural resources should not offset agencies' gross costs, unless the full costs of the natural resources sold are recognized. Second, it suggests that some natural resource assets -- in particular, those where the asset is held for remunerative operations or sale -- should be recognized on the Balance Sheet, and not solely in the stewardship report; this would also allow the full costs of natural resources that are sold to be recognized on the Statement of Net Cost. Finally, the comments suggest that the Government develop basic data where it has valuable resources that it intends to sell or manage for remunerative purposes.

V. Implications of the Suggested Reporting Principles

In addition to studying the various reporting options of natural resources, the task force was also instructed to identify the related impacts on existing FASAB standards based on the options and to identify existing laws and regulations that affect reporting information about natural resources.

Impact on Current FASAB Standards

SFFAS No. 7, *Accounting for Revenue and Other Financing Sources and Concepts for Reconciling Budgetary and Financial Accounting* provides that exchange revenue should generally be reported on the Statement of Net Cost of Operations of the agency earning the revenue. However, the Statement makes an exception to this principle for entities recognizing virtually no costs in connection with earning the revenue that it collects (e.g., Outer Continental Shelf revenue collected by the Minerals Management Service). Based on the work performed by the task force, it is the view of some of the task force members that the Outer Continental Shelf rents and royalties are not substantially different from other natural resource revenues and other exchange revenues.

With the exception of the fact that the acreage in question is underwater, MMS's resource management responsibilities over the Outer Continental Shelf are very similar to the resource management responsibilities of the Bureau of Land Management. While MMS royalty collections may be larger in size than certain other natural resource inflows, in substance they have much in common with other resources.

Various task force members believe that revenues earned from the sale of natural resources should be matched against its costs by the agency that collects that revenue and by the government as a whole. This is to ensure that the proceeds the government derives from its stewardship over natural resources are more clearly reported.

The task force also recommends that the Board take into account the following implementation considerations, if it does agree to revise SFFAS No. 7:

- changes necessary to agency/program system requirements,
- possible use of pilot programs, and
- allowing adequate time to implement the revisions.

Legal/Regulatory Considerations

In the course of its work the task force learned about the many statutory and regulatory authorities that affect the value of Federal natural resources and the revenues the Federal Government receives when they are conveyed to the private sector. For many resources, there are statutory requirements that require the Government to use competitive market processes to determine the price at which Federal resources will be conveyed. In general, such requirements have contributed to the development of management procedures that have promoted receipt of revenues that reflect the market value of the resources.

There are, however, a number of resources for which the statutory requirements limit the Federal Government's ability to develop management practices that assure receipt of market value. For example, there has been extended controversy about such limitations regarding mining claims and patents under the General Mining Law of 1872 and grazing permits under Public Rangelands Improvement Act of 1978.

VI. Indian Natural Resource Assets

The Bureau of Indian Affairs (BIA) currently administers more than 54 million acres of land that the Federal Government holds in trust for Indian tribes and individuals. The Indian trust funds are managed by Interior's Office of Special Trustee, Office of the Secretary. (Prior to FY 1996 the BIA managed the trust funds). Some of the funds belong to individual Indians others belong to tribes. The Federal Government manages the funds in a trust arrangement. Trust responsibilities include management of forest lands, development of agricultural and range lands, leasing mineral rights, protecting water and land rights, preparation and administration of probates, and maintaining land ownership and lease income records. Each year, trust lands generate significant resource revenue for beneficiaries, including about $550 million in agricultural production and $150 million in mineral royalties.

Legal Background

Lands under the jurisdiction of the BIA which are held in trust for tribes and individuals were placed in trust by treaties, statutes (e.g., the General Allotment Act), and Executive Orders. Resources on these lands (e.g., minerals, sand and gravel) are managed for the benefit of tribes and individual Indians. Neither the lands held in trust nor the resources associated with these lands are Federal Government assets. In contrast, the Government does own and the BIA administers about 635 thousand acres, with schools, hospitals, offices, roads, etc., which are accounted for in the same manner as other Federal lands and resources.

Reporting on Indian Trust Assets

The Government's responsibility for the trust funds is of a fiduciary nature. This has been confirmed in FASAB Interpretation No. 1 discussed below. The Federal government as a trustee has responsibility for managing certain assets on behalf of tribes and individual Indians, but does not have ownership of either the trust assets or the proceeds from the assets. Historically, a portion of the annual flow from some of these trust funds has been included in the *Budget of the United States Government*. This treatment is being corrected to properly exclude non-Federal assets from the *Budget of the United States Government*.

In addition, revenue generated from Indian trust assets is accounted for on behalf of the tribes and individual Indians. The Mineral Management Service generally acts a collection agency for oil and gas and other mineral resources. The Office of Trust Funds Management has the lead role in performing the accounting. BIA's costs of managing and selling natural resources from trust lands are generally part of the costs of managing other resources and carrying out its mission.

FASAB Interpretation No. 1

In 1997 the FASAB issued Interpretation No. 1, *Interpretation of Federal*

Financial Accounting Standards -- Reporting on Indian Trust Funds in General Purpose Financial Reports of the Department of the Interior and in the Consolidated Financial Statements of the United States Government: an interpretation of SFFAS No.7. The Interpretation deals with what information about Indian trust funds should be included in the general-purpose financial report of the Department of Interior and of the United States Government. Interpretation No. 1 specifically addresses the question on whether the assets and activities of the Indian trust funds should be reported in the Department of Interior's general purpose financial statements.

The Interpretation states that the assets, liabilities and operating transactions of the Indian trust funds are not part of the Department of Interior and should not be included in the Balance Sheet, Statement of Net Cost, and Statement of Changes in Financial Position of the Department or of the United States Government. However, the Department of Interior does have a fiduciary responsibility for the Indian trust assets and is required to report on them in the Department's footnotes to the basic financial statements as stated in SFFAS No. 7, *Accounting for Revenue and Other Financing Sources*, paragraphs 83-87.

Additional Suggested Reporting

Some members of the task force believe that the footnote disclosures discussed in Interpretation 1 should contain sufficient information to provide an understanding of the fiduciary relationship and the assets and revenues involved. One member of the task force from Interior also believes that there must be more detailed reporting to tribes and individual Indians regarding trust lands and resources, including information on earned revenue and, if estimable, quantity and value of natural resources available for sale. When appropriate, reports to trust beneficiaries should also address financial management systems and internal accounting and administrative controls.

Appendix A. Reporting by Individual Resource

Appendix A contains detailed information for eight natural resource related programs managed by the Federal government. Each program section contains: general and legal background information; a description of the different "stages" of management processes; current reporting policies; and issues relating to the availability and existence of data. The following eight natural resource related programs are presented in the appendix.

- Timber
- Outer Continental Shelf Oil and Gas
- Leasable Minerals - Solid
- Leasable Minerals - Fluid
- Locatable Minerals
- Mineral Materials
- Grazing Uses
- Electromagnetic Spectrum (Airwaves)

Timber

A. Background

1. General Information and Legal Background

Ownership: Ownership of timber resources is based on the status and ownership of the land, including the trees thereon. Most of the timber on Federal land is in fee simple ownership. Approximately 73 percent of the 191 million acres of the National Forests, managed by the USDA Forest Service is considered forested. Of this forested land, 35 percent is available for regularly scheduled timber harvest and about ½ of 1 percent of those trees are harvested in any one-year. Of the Bureau of Land Management's (BLM) 264 million acres, about 47 million areas are classified as forestland, although only about 4 million acres outside of Alaska are actually classified as "productive" (capable of producing timber). Even though BLM in Alaska has 7 million acres that are capable of producing timber, most of this forestland is either inaccessible or too far from established markets to make timber harvest feasible.

Legal Authority: Management of Federal forestland is authorized by various statutes. For the USDA Forest Service (FS), these include the Organic Administration Act (Organic Act) of 1897 (16 USC 475); the Multiple-Use, Sustained-Yield Act of 1960 (16 USC 528-531); the Forest and Rangeland Renewable Resources Planning Act (RPA) of 1974 (16 USC 1600 et seq.); and the National Forest Management Act (NFMA) of 1976 (16 USC et seq.). For the USDI Bureau of Land Management, the applicable laws are the Federal Land Policy and Management Act (FLPMA) of 1976 (43 USC 1701 et seq.) and the Oregon and California (O&C) Grant Lands Act of 1937 (43 USC 1181). DoD conducts natural resource management activities under the Sikes Act (16 USC 670).

Sale of Timber: The Organic Act, RPA, and NFMA authorize Timber sales from National Forests. The regulations for Forest Service timber sales are in 36 CFR 223. The sale and disposal of timber from BLM managed land is authorized by the Material Disposal Act (30 USC 601 et seq.) and the O&C Act. The regulations for BLM timber sales are in 43 CFR 5400. Timber sales on DoD lands are authorized through 10 USC 2665.

National Forests and BLM public lands are managed under a "multiple use" mandate pursuant to the Multiple-Use, Sustained-Yield Act and FLPMA, respectively. This mandate and other factors cause timber sales to be part of a complex and integrated strategy to provide public values and benefits while maintaining or improving ecological integrity. In planning for timber sales, agencies conduct detailed, project-level environmental analyses and documentation pursuant to the National Environmental Policy

Act. In addition, extensive public participation is involved in the Forest Service and BLM timber sale planning processes.

Valuation: Prior to the advertisement of a timber sale, a timber appraisal is conducted in accordance with established agency policy and procedures. The appraisal is used to establish the minimum bid. Bids are solicited for each contract, and timber is sold to the highest bidder.

2. **Description of "Stages" for Resource**

Conveyed: Generally, conveyance of the timber resource takes place when the timber is paid for and severed from the ground in accordance with a timber sale contract. In the case of the Forest Service and Bureau of Land Management, conveyance occurs when the above conditions are met and when the timber is removed from the contract area.

Available for Sale: The amount of timber available for sale within an administrative unit (National Forest, BLM Resource Area, DoD installation) is generally stated in a land management plan for that administrative unit. The Federal sustained-yield mandate provides that the government not harvest more timber than is produced (through growth) over time. On much of the Forest Service and BLM productive forestland, the management emphasis or "highest and best use" is not necessarily timber, but rather a multitude of other values and benefits like recreation, aesthetics, water quality, wildlife (including threatened and endangered species) habitat, wilderness, and other values. The DoD actively manages its forests first to facilitate the military mission. Other uses, such as wildlife habitat, biological diversity, watershed protection, and timber, are secondary benefits from DoD forestlands. All agencies generally manage the forest for a multitude of values and benefits while maintaining the ecological integrity of the forest.

Administratively and Legislatively Withdrawn: For DoD, many areas are administratively withdrawn from timber harvest for military mission-related reasons. Many forested areas on Forest Service and BLM lands are legislatively withdrawn from timber harvest (e.g., wilderness areas under the Wilderness Act). Other areas are administratively withdrawn from timber harvest to protect sensitive areas or to enhance other values.

Unknown and Undiscovered Resource: Information regarding the extent of the forest and amount of timber available varies widely across agencies and administrative units. On some areas, very specific and accurate information is available on the timber resource while, on other areas, very little is known. This is a function of differing management emphases and funding levels. The Forest Service's Forest Inventory and Analysis (FIA) collects information at a course scale that can be used at the national or regional level to estimate timber levels on all land, including Federal land. However, this information is not specific enough to be used in the management of a specific administrative unit.

B.   Current Reporting

1.   **Asset Recognition:** <u>BLM</u>: Timber is recognized as an asset in agencies' accounting records at the time a timber sale contract is awarded. <u>DoD</u>: Timber is recognized as an asset when a contract is signed for the sale of that timber. <u>FS</u>: Currently, FS does not recognize timber as an asset on the financial statements. Department of Energy (<u>DOE</u>): Energy recognizes timber as an asset. The value recorded each year is based on the historical cost of the timber management program, and the cost for the current year is calculated at year-end and added to the asset account.

2.   **Revenue Recognition:** <u>BLM</u> : Revenues are recognized upon receipt of advance payments or other periodic payments in accordance with the terms of the timber sale contract. <u>DoD</u>: Revenue from timber sales is recognized when proceeds from the sale of timber are collected. Advance payments received are recognized as unearned revenue and are recorded as a liability until the payment is earned. At such time, the revenue is recognized and the liability reduced. <u>FS</u>: Revenues are recognized as deferred exchange revenue and allocated to revenue monthly based on timber harvested and removed during the month. <u>DOE</u>: Energy recognizes revenues upon receipt of the payments from timber sale contracts.

3.   **Cost Recognition**

(a)   **Cost of Resources Sold:** Timber production occurs over long periods of time and in concert with multiple land management objectives. Costs associated with timber production are not matched against timber sale revenues. <u>DOE</u>: Energy also recognizes the depletion of the asset in a contra asset account (an allowance for timber depletion). The calculation is based on the estimate of net merchantable volume of timber, which is calculated by the foresters, and the net "balance to deplete" of the timber asset, which is the net value of the asset account and the contra asset account.

(b)   **Cost of selling:** Administrative costs associated with timber sales are recognized in the period incurred. Although a portion of the proceeds emanating from certain types of timber sales can be retained by the managing agency and, in some instances, can be used for timber sale administration, much of the cost of timber sales is borne by agencies' operating appropriations. The DoD supplements most of the costs from timber sale proceeds, but may use operating appropriations if necessary.

(c)   **Cost of Management:** Management costs are recognized in the period incurred. Although a portion of the proceeds emanating from timber sales can be retained by the managing agency and, in some instances, can be used for managing timber production and sales, much of this activity is funded through the agencies' operating appropriations. The DoD supplements most of the costs from timber sale proceeds, but may use operating appropriations if necessary.

(d)   **Transfers of Revenue/Distribution of Receipts:** In general, receipts are distributed in accordance with the laws regulating the specific lands from which timber is sold. Proceeds from timber sales are collected by the managing agency and distributed to some combination of states, counties, the general fund of the Treasury, the Reclamation Fund, and other funds/entities as the various laws require. Typically, the managing agency is allowed by law to retain some portion of timber sale receipts for both general and specific purposes. The Forest Service reports these transfers and distributions as costs on the Statement of Net Cost and as transfers-out on the Statement of Changes in Net Position.

4.   Other Reporting

(a)   **Footnote Disclosure:** <u>BLM</u>: Agency financial statements include footnote disclosures covering both unmatured portions of timber sale contracts and the liability account for deferred credits (revenues).

(b) **Stewardship Reporting:** Stewardship reporting currently excludes natural resources.

C. Availability and Existence of Data

Data is available on the approximate acres of forestlands. Forest management planning data is available. Data is available on numbers of contracts, quantities offered, quantities sold, quantities removed, revenues collected, and the disposition of revenues. However, no value can be determined for timber owned by the Federal Government in its entirety.

Outer Continental Shelf Oil and Gas

A.   Background

1. General Information and Legal Background

Ownership: The Outer Continental Shelf (OCS) consists of over 1.4 billion acres of submerged lands seaward of State jurisdiction. The Submerged Lands Act of 1953 granted states rights to the natural resources within 3 nautical miles of the coastline, except for the Gulf of Mexico coasts of Texas and Florida, where State jurisdiction extends for 3 marine leagues. The Federal Government manages the rights to oil, gas, and other minerals on the OCS. The Government issues leases that convey an exclusive right to explore for and develop oil and gas on the OCS, and maintain a royalty interest in any production saved, removed, or sold from a lease. Over 27 million acres are currently under active lease, and the OCS accounts for over 27% of the natural gas and 20% of the oil produced in the United States.

Legal Authority: The Outer Continental Shelf Lands Act, as amended, and the Federal Oil and Gas Royalty Management Act, as amended, are the primary legal authorities for managing oil and gas resources on the OCS, though authority for certain management activities resides in a number of other statutes as well. The Secretary of the Interior has jurisdiction over energy and mineral development on the OCS and has delegated much of that authority to the Minerals Management Service (MMS).

Sale of Leases: MMS conducts auctions for OCS leases under competitive sealed-bidding procedures and evaluates the high bids on each block to determine if each bid meets or exceeds bid adequacy criteria. Although various alternative bidding systems have been tested, MMS generally offers leases with fixed annual rentals and royalty rates (usually one-eighth or one-sixth) and with a cash bonus as the bid variable. Primary lease terms range from 5 to 10 years, at which time the lease expires unless the lessee is producing or conducting drilling or well-reworking operations, subject to regulations. The lease remains in force for as long as it's producing, which could be decades.

Valuation: The majority of OCS revenues come from three sources: cash bonuses, royalty revenues, and rentals. The following table summarizes these revenues.

OCS Mineral Revenues		
Revenue Type	**1998**	**1953-1998**
Royalties	$2.7 billion	$62 billion
Bonuses	$1.3 billion	$61 billion
Rentals	$258 million	$1.7 billion

MMS relies on its competitive bidding process and bid evaluation procedures to ensure the receipt of fair value for OCS leases. Royalties are generally a fixed percentage of gross proceeds to the lessee from the sale of lease production.

2. Description of Phases

Conveyed: Conveyance occurs when the Government issues a lease for exclusive rights to explore for and develop oil and gas on the OCS. In return, the Government receives a cash bonus at the time of lease issuance, annual rental payments until production begins, and a production royalty. Leased acreage returns to the Government's inventory when a lessee relinquishes a lease, the primary lease term expires and the lessee is not conducting operations that would extend the lease term, or the Government cancels a lease pursuant to the authorities in the OCS Lands Act.

Available for Sale: All OCS acreage not specifically withdrawn or under lease is potentially available for leasing. The Secretary of the Interior prepares a 5-Year Oil and Gas Leasing Program that identifies the size, timing, and location of possible lease sales. Interior consults extensively with States and other stakeholders in preparing the plan. Only acreage specifically identified in this plan may be offered for sale.

In addition, each individual lease sale has its own public planning process. This process could result in cancellation or delay of a sale or a reduction in the acreage to be offered for lease, but it cannot add acreage that was not included in the 5-Year Program.

Administratively and Legislatively Withdrawn: Both the Administration and Congress can withdraw portions of the OCS from the 5-year planning process, and thus prevent them from being leased. Withdrawals can occur for policy reasons or to reserve an area for other uses.

Underscored Resources: Much of the OCS remains unexplored and is believed to contain substantial volumes of undiscovered resources. The most recent national assessment of undiscovered, conventionally recoverable resources on the OCS estimated that 186.3 – 369.2 trillion cubic feet of natural gas and 37.1 – 55.3 billion barrels of oil remain undiscovered.

B.   Current Reporting

1.   **Asset Recognition:** Currently, oil and gas resources on the Outer Continental Shelf are not recognized as assets in the MMS Annual Financial Statements.

2.   **Revenue Recognition:** Currently, the MMS Annual Financial Statements and DOI Consolidated Financial Statements recognize receipts from the initial leasing of OCS tracts in the period the lease sale is held. For leases that have entered into production, royalty receipts are recognized in the period the oil or gas production is saved, removed, or sold by the lessee. The receipts are presented in a Statement of Custodial Activity, but are not considered revenue to DOI. The receipts are considered revenue in the Government wide financial statements.

3.   **Cost Recognition**

    (a)   **Cost of Resources Sold:** There is currently no reporting of the cost of oil and gas sold.

    (b)   **Cost of selling:** Currently, the MMS recognizes all costs associated with lease sales, royalty collections and disbursements, and other activities in support of OCS production.

    (c)   **Cost of Management:** Currently, separate management costs are not recognized for OCS oil and gas resources.

    (d)   **Transfers of Revenue/Distribution of Receipts:** Under section 8(g) of the OCSLA, MMS does distribute receipts from OCS leases to non-Federal agencies. In 1997 MMS transferred over $116 million of OCS revenues to states.

4. **Other Reporting**

    (a)   **Footnote Disclosure:** None

    (b)   **Stewardship Reporting:** None

C.   **Availability and Existence of Data**

The data identified in the reporting section of this paper is generally available on an annual basis, with the following exceptions:

• Net present value of reserves — No such estimates are currently made for the OCS. However, if one makes a number of economic assumptions (e.g., future prices, costs and timing of production), uncertain estimates are feasible.

• Volume and net economic value of resources in the 5-Year Oil and Gas Leasing Program — These estimates are made during the preparation of each 5-Year Program and are not updated until a new program is prepared (roughly every 5 years).

• Undiscovered resources — These estimates are made periodically.

Leasable Minerals (Solid)

A. Background

1. General Information and Legal Background

Leasable minerals are broadly segregated into two general categories based on the physical properties of the minerals, and as such, are discussed separately. Fluid minerals are those minerals that generally occur in a fluid or gaseous state and include oil, gas, and geothermal resources. These fluid minerals are discussed in a section entitled "Leasable Minerals (Fluid)." Solid leasable minerals are those minerals that generally occur in a solid state and include coal, oil shale, asphalt, sulfur, phosphate, potassium, sodium, gilsonite, and other minerals.

The Bureau of Land Management is responsible for managing on-shore leasing and lease operations. The Minerals Management Service is responsible for off-shore leasing and lease operations as well as for collecting and distributing mineral revenues for both on-shore and off-shore minerals.

Ownership: The Federal Government is responsible for managing the mineral estate that underlies approximately 264 million acres of Federal ownership and an additional 300 million acres of mineral rights on split estate lands for which the surface has been conveyed. The government transfers title to certain minerals to private entities through leases. The lessee is required to pay an annual per-acre rental fee to hold the lease, as well as a royalty based on sales value when the mineral has been severed.

Legal Authority: The primary legislation governing leasable minerals is the Mineral Leasing Act of 1920, as amended. This legislation separated mineral fuels and fertilizer minerals (oil, gas, oil shales, asphalt, phosphate, potassium, and sodium) from the General Mining Law of 1872. The Mineral Leasing Act was amended by the Federal Coal Leasing Amendment Act of 1976, which provided for coal to be leased competitively through regional leasing or leasing by application.

The Federal Land Policy and Management Act of 1976 requires that the United States receive market value for the use of the public lands and their resources unless otherwise provided by statute. In practice, market value for solid leasable mineral is the combined value of future royalties, which are established by the Mineral Leasing Act, and a competitive lease bonus payment that is bid by the prospective lessee and is payable upon lease issuance.

Leasing of Minerals: The most common form of Federal leasing is known as "competitive leasing," which provides an opportunity for any interested party to competitively bid for a Federal lease. Prospecting permits and noncompetitive preference right leases may be issued for some noncoal solid minerals. Most leases have terms that require diligent development of the resource, with rents and royalties being paid for the right to hold the lease and mine the Federal resources.

Mineral leases are issued for an initial period of 20 years and are subject to readjustment or renewal at 10- and 20-year increments. Changes in royalty and rental rates, as well as revisions to other terms and conditions of the lease, can be made or attached during the readjustment or renewal of a lease.

Leasing of coal and noncoal minerals has occurred on about 1.1 million acres of mineral rights on Federal and split-estate private lands.

Valuation: Competitive leasing provides an opportunity for more than one party to bid on a lease tract. Non-competitive leases are awarded based on the mineral discovery from a prospecting permit or as a modification to an existing lease.

In all cases, solid mineral leases are sold only at or above the government's estimation of market value. Through a lease sale, the public may bid on mineral resources offered for competitive lease. The highest bid is awarded the lease. Lands leased through lease modification procedures require that the lessee pay a payment in lieu of a bonus bid. The lease also requires payment of an annual per-acre rental fee and may require advance royalties.

2. **Description of "Stages" for Resource**

Conveyed (Granted Rights): The government receives rentals, bonus bids, and other payments when leases are issued. Payment for the mineral resources in the form of royalties occurs when the mineral is severed and/or sold. Royalties on the sales value of resource production are paid at least quarterly to the United States through the Minerals Management Service.

Available for Sale (Lease): Not all public lands are available for mineral exploration or leasing. There is a rigorous land use planning process through which all public lands are reviewed for potential leasing. The land use plan must address multiple use, sustained yield, protection of critical environmental areas, application of specific unsuitability criteria, and coordination with other government agencies.

Administratively and Legislatively Withdrawn: Some Federal lands are closed to mineral leasing by legislative withdrawal and/or administrative decisions reached through the land use planning process.

Unknown/Undiscovered: The Federal Government does not attempt to identify the magnitude of leasable resources through exploration or prospecting. In some cases the agency has rough estimates of reserves, but many factors influence the mineability and marketability of leasable resources, including environmental constraints, world markets, and changes in technology.

B. **Current Reporting**

1. **Asset Recognition:** The value of solid leasable minerals is currently not recognized as an asset in the financial records of Federal agencies.

2. **Revenue Recognition:** Revenues generated from mineral leases are recognized at the time lease payments or royalties are collected.

3. **Cost Recognition**

    (a)   **Cost of Resources Sold:** Solid minerals are not currently recognized as an asset in agencies' financial records. As such, there is there is no asset to be removed at the time of sale.

    (b)   **Cost of selling:** Administration of the solid mineral leasing program is funded through operating appropriations. The cost of selling is recognized in the period incurred.

(c) **Cost of Management:** Management of the solid mineral leasing program is funded through operating appropriations. The cost of management is recognized in the period incurred.

(d) **Transfers of Revenue/Distribution of Receipts:** Revenues are not retained by the managing agency. They are distributed annually to the General Fund of the Treasury and to the states and counties from which the minerals were extracted.

4. Other Reporting

(a) **Footnote Disclosure:** None

(b) **Stewardship Reporting:** None

C. Availability and Existence of Data

Some data is available at the time a lease is executed, such as the number of leases, revenues generated from those leases, the distribution of lease revenues, and, for some minerals, the quantities extracted. However, no value can be determined for mineral rights owned by the Federal Government in their entirety. The quantities of leasable mineral reserves that would determine future production potential at identified deposits are generally unknown. Furthermore, estimates of the volumes of minerals that might exist in undiscovered deposits on Federal lands are not reliable enough to report on the face of the financial statements.

Leasable Minerals (Fluid)

A.   Background

1.   General Information and Legal Background

As previously stated, fluid minerals are those that generally occur in a fluid or gaseous state and include oil, gas, and geothermal energy.

Ownership: The BLM has exclusive jurisdiction over the mineral rights for about 264 million acres of public lands (with approximately one-third of this area being in Alaska). The BLM also managers an additional 300 million acres of subsurface mineral rights reserved by the Federal Government.

The management objective of the oil and gas program is to foster and encourage the exploration for and development of Federal and Indian oil and gas resources, to receive a fair return to the public and Indian lessors for those resources in an environmentally acceptable manner, and to provide for conservation of fluid mineral resources in a manner that is responsive to the Nation's economic and security needs and in conformance with the principles of balanced multiple-use management.

Legal Authority: The Mineral Leasing Act of 1920, as amended, the Mineral Leasing Act for Acquired Lands of 1947, the National Environmental Policy Act of 1969, the Federal Land Policy and Management Act of 1976, the Federal Oil and Gas Royalty Act of 1982, and the Federal Onshore Oil and Gas Reform Act of 1987 are the primary authorities under which the BLM leases and supervises oil and gas operations. The regulations are contained in Title 43 of the Code of Federal Regulations.

Leasing: Onshore oil and gas leasing is accomplished under competitive procedures. Current leasing procedures were established by the Federal Onshore Oil and Gas Leasing Reform Act of 1987 (30 U.S.C. 226, et seq.).

Valuation:

-   *Bonus Bids:* In FY 1996, 2,477 competitive leases covering 1,589,795 acres with $31,979,336 in accepted bonus bids, along with 898 non-competitive oil and gas leases covering 933,763 acres, were issued.

-   *Royalties*: In calendar year 1996 for Federal onshore lands, oil royalty income rose 20.2 percent to $232.4 million, while gas royalty income rose 23.9 percent to $309.9 million. Regarding geothermal energy, during 1996, MMS collected approximately

$19.9 million in royalties from geothermal leases on Federal lands in California, Nevada, and Utah. In 1997, approximately $20.8 million in royalties from geothermal leases was collected for these same 3 areas.

2. Description of "Stages" for Resource

Conveyed: Conveyance occurs when the government issues a lease for the exclusive right to explore for and develop oil and gas on the lands for which the government holds the mineral rights. The lessee is then responsible to remit to the government the following types of payments:

- *Bonuses:* Through the competitive bidding process, the bonus represents the cash amount successfully bid to win the rights to a lease.

- *Rents:* A rent schedule is established at the time a lease is issued. Rents are annual payments, normally a fixed dollar amount per acre, required to preserve the rights to a lease.

- *Royalties:* A royalty is due when production begins. Royalty payments represent a stated share or percentage of the value of the oil and gas produced. The royalty may be an established minimum value or a flat, step-scale, or sliding-scale rate. A step-scale royalty rate increases by steps as the average production on the lease increases. A sliding-scale royalty rate is based on average production and applies to all production on the lease.

Available for Sale (Lease): Not all public lands are available for oil and gas exploration or leasing. There is a rigorous land use planning process through which all public lands are reviewed for potential leasing. The land use plan must address multiple use, sustained yield, protection of critical environmental areas, application of specific unsuitability criteria, and coordination with other government agencies.

Administratively and Legislatively Withdrawn: Portions of Federal lands are withdrawn or otherwise closed to leasing and/or development.

Unknown/Undiscovered: In general, the Federal Government does not attempt to identify the magnitude of leasable oil and gas resources through exploration. In some cases, the government has rough estimates of reserves, but many factors influence the availability of the oil and gas resources, including environmental constraints, world markets, and changes in technology.[6]

---

[6] The most recent USGS National Assessment of undiscovered, conventionally recoverable resources on onshore Federal lands

B.   Current Reporting

1. **Asset Recognition:** On-shore oil and gas deposits are not currently recognized as assets in the financial records of government agencies.

2. **Revenue Recognition:** Revenues emanating from oil and gas leases are recognized at the time lease payments (bonuses, rents, and royalties) are collected.

3. **Cost Recognition**

    (a)   **Cost of Resources Sold:** Oil and gas deposits are not currently recorded as assets, so there is no resource cost to match against revenues.

    (b)   **Cost of selling:** The cost of administering on-shore oil and gas leasing activities is currently recognized in the period incurred.

    (c)   **Cost of Management:** The cost of managing the on-shore oil and gas program is currently recognized in the period incurred.

    (d)   **Transfers of Revenue/Distribution of Receipts:** Revenues collected by the managing agency are generally not retained by that agency. They are distributed annually in various percentages to the General Fund of the Treasury, the Reclamation Fund, and to the states and counties from which the minerals were extracted in accordance with the laws applicable to the lands upon which the oil and gas lease resides.

4. **Other Reporting**

    (a)   **Footnote Disclosure:** None.

    (b)   **Stewardship Reporting:** None.

C. Availability and Existence of Data

---

estimated 34 - 97 trillion cubic feet of natural gas and 4 to 13 billion barrels of oil remain undiscovered. Furthermore, an additional 72 to 202 trillion feed of gas was estimated to be contained in unconventional gas deposits (excluding coalbed gas) on onshore Federal Land. Coalbed gas deposits on Federal Lands were estimated to contain 13 to 20 trillion feet of gas. These estimates are general magnitudes of undiscovered volumes of onshore oil and gas. The USGS periodically assesses the undiscovered onshore oil and gas resources for the entire United States. The USGS then allocates, in a publication, that portion of the resources that it believes should be applied to Federal lands.

Certain data is available on the number of leases, including revenues generated, the distribution of revenues, and the quantities of the oil and gas extracted. However, no value can reasonably be determined for mineral rights owned by the Federal Government in their entirety.

Locatable Minerals

A.   Background

1.   General Information and Legal Background

<u>Ownership</u>: The class of economic minerals known as "locatable" minerals make up a significant portion of the "economic" minerals under government control. This class includes precious metals, ferrous metals, light metals, base metals, precious and semi-precious gemstones, and a vast array of industrial minerals. Nineteen states are open to the operation of the General Mining Law of 1872, as amended, which creates this class of minerals.

<u>Legal Authority</u>: Locatable minerals are made available under the Mining Law of 1872 (30 USC 22, et seq.), the Federal Land Policy and Management Act (43 USC 1732 and 1744), and continuing Appropriations Acts. On acquired lands, locatable minerals are leased.

<u>Disposal/Sale Mechanisms</u>: A citizen who makes a self-initiated discovery of a deposit of valuable minerals and who records a mining claim with the Federal Government has the right to produce the mineral deposit, subject to compliance with applicable Federal, state, and local health, safety, and environmental laws.

Recordation of a mining claim requires payment of a location fee, administrative costs, and payment of the annual maintenance fee. The annual maintenance fee is paid each year in advance. Initial recordation with the Federal Government requires advance payment of location, maintenance fee, and administrative fees (service charges) in the amount of $135.00. Maintenance fees currently run $100 per claim per year. Location fees are $25 per claim. Administrative fees are $10 per mining claim. Subsequent years require the payment of the maintenance fee of $100. Claimants who hold 10 claims or less are considered "small miners" and have the option to file a waiver of the $100 fee. There are approximately 320,000 mining claims of record.

The term "location" is used to identify posting of a location notice and marking the boundaries of a claim [*Smith v. Union Oil Co., 135 P 966 (1913), affirmed 249 US 337*]. The following Federal requirements for location must be accomplished:

1. The location must be distinctly marked on the ground so its boundaries can be readily traced.

2. The location notice must contain (a) the name or names of the locators, (b) the date of the location, and (c) a description of the claim(s)' location by reference to some natural or permanent monument that will identify the claim.

Valuation: There are no up-to-date or reliable estimates of the value of in-place reserves.

2. **Description of "Stages" for Resource**

Conveyed (Discovery, Location and Recordation, and Patenting): Citizens have standing permission to go on Federal lands that are not withdrawn from the mining law, to prospect for locatable mineral deposits. Discovery of a valuable mineral grants to the discoverer the conditional right to develop the minerals.

When a prospector locates a mining claim, the claim must be recorded with the county pursuant to state law and with the Federal Government within 90 days of location pursuant to Federal law. The validity of a claim is determined using the "Prudent Man [aka Person] Test." This test states, ". . . where minerals have been found and the evidence is of such a character that a person of ordinary prudence would be justified in further expenditure of his labor and means, with a reasonable prospect of success, in developing a valuable mine, the requirements of the statutes have been met."

A mining claimant can seek full fee title to the land by filing for patent (deed) to the mining claim. There are application/administrative fees paid for a mineral survey and the actual patent application. When the administrative processing of the application has reached a certain point, the purchase price (set by statute at $2.50/acre for placer claims or $5.00/acre for lode claims) is paid. If examination demonstrates the existence of a valuable mineral deposit, the title to the land and minerals passes to the mining claimant. Currently, there is a moratorium on accepting patent applications. The government receives no royalties from the production of locatable minerals.

Available for Exploration, Development, Production and Reclamation: There is no requirement to apply for a patent. Exploration and mining can be conducted to completion without the issuance of a patent.

Exploration and mining operations are subject to government review and approval, and must meet Federal and State laws. Financial guarantees are required of an operator to ensure reclamation is completed upon disturbed lands. No charges for either approval or oversight of activities are assessed of an operator; however, the BLM is currently preparing cost recovery regulations.

Administratively and Legislatively Withdrawn: The current estimate of lands withdrawn from locatable mineral production on the public domain land base is approximately 330 million acres out of a total of 564 million acres. No reliable value of withdrawn minerals has been developed.

Unknown and Undiscovered Resources: There are no reliable estimates of the value of unknown or undiscovered resource.

B.   Current Reporting

1.   **Asset Recognition:** The aggregate value of locatable minerals on or underlying the public lands is not recognized as an asset in agencies' accounting records.

2.   **Revenue Recognition:** Revenues emanating from mining claim location and maintenance fees are recognized in the period in which they are collected.

3.   **Cost Recognition**

   (a)   **Cost of Resources Sold:** The value of locatable minerals removed from the public lands is not matched with revenues received.

   (b)   **Cost of selling:** Costs associated with program administration are recognized in the period incurred and are matched against revenues received for fee collections.

   (c)   **Cost of Management:** The cost of managing the locatable minerals program is funded through fee collections. This cost is recognized in the period incurred and matched against revenues.

   (d)   **Transfers of Revenue/Distribution of Receipts:** Fee revenues emanating from the locatable minerals program are collected by the managing agency, but are appropriated by Congress.

4.   **Other Reporting**

   (a)   **Footnote Disclosure:** None

   (b)   **Stewardship Reporting:** None

C.   Availability and Existence of Data

Data is available on the number of mining claims and the revenues generated. Although data is diverse, no mandatory National reporting system for privately developed production data (e.g., produced reserves) or privately produced resource data (e.g., exploration information) exists.

Mineral Materials

A. **Background**

1. **General Information and Legal Background**

Ownership. Mineral materials include various common minerals such as sand, gravel, and stones that are considered part of the mineral estate owned by the Federal Government. The Federal Government manages these minerals on public lands and other lands under the jurisdiction of the government.

Legal authority. The Materials Acts of July 31, 1947 (61 Stat. 681), as amended, authorizes the disposal of mineral materials through sale contracts to private users. Disposal is also authorized through free use to non-profit organizations if the material is not to be used for commercial purposes, as well as to governmental entities.

Sale of Mineral Materials. Sale of mineral materials may not be made at less than market value as determined by an appraisal. Sales must be made on a competitive basis unless it can be shown that there is no competitive interest. Sales are made from either exclusive site used by one operator or nonexclusive sites (community pits or common use areas) for use by more than one operator.

Negotiated sales are generally for less than 100,000 cubic yards of mineral materials. The maximum duration of the contract term is for 5 years, with a one-time extension of 1 year.

Competitive sales are for mineral material disposal of over 100,000 cubic yards or where there is competitive interest even for smaller sales. The maximum term is for 10 years, with a one-time extension of one year.

Valuation. Valuation is made by conducting an appraisal of the material to be sold utilizing the Uniform Appraisal Standards for Federal Land Acquisition (602 DM 1.3).

2. **Description of "Stages" for Resource**

Conveyed: Conveyance of the right to remove Federal mineral materials is made at the time a contract or permit is issued. No mineral materials can be removed without a prior payment for the amount to be removed, except in cases where free use conveys a right to a governmental subdivision or non-profit organization to remove mineral materials without payment.

Available for Sale: Mineral materials on public lands are generally available for purchase under established procedures unless otherwise prohibited by law or withdrawn because of an agency's land use plan decisions. Limited assessments of the total quantities of mineral materials on the public lands have been made as a part of agencies' resource management planning initiatives.

<u>Administratively and Legislatively Withdrawn</u>: The government does not issue mineral material sales from lands identified in the land management planning process as unsuitable for such mineral development. The BLM also cannot sell mineral materials from lands encumbered by unpatented mining claims.

<u>Unknown / Undiscovered</u>: While mineral materials are generally of widespread surface occurrence, their usage varies with the degree of economic development of an area, with the greatest demand generally occurring during periods of high economic activity or infrastructure development. Demand for a material depends on the type of usage contemplated. To explore and test a deposit to determine the quality and quantity of available material, operators can obtain permits from the government. Such a permit does not convey to the permittee a preference right to a contract.

B.   Current Reporting

1. **Asset Recognition:** Mineral materials are not currently recognized as an asset in the financial records of government agencies.

2. **Revenue Recognition:** Revenues from the sale of mineral materials are recognized in the period that payments are received by the government according to the payment schedule authorized by the executed agreement between the contractee and the government.

3. **Cost Recognition**

    (a)   **Cost of Resources Sold:** Mineral materials are not currently recorded as an asset in the financial records of government agencies. Therefore, no cost is recognized at the time of sale.

    (b)   **Cost of selling:** The cost of selling are recognized in the period incurred.

    (c)   **Cost of Management:** The costs of managing the mineral materials program are recognized in the period incurred.

    (d)   **Transfers of Revenue/Distribution of Receipts:** Receipts from the sale of mineral materials are generally not retained by the managing agency. They are distributed annually to the general fund of the Treasury, to states and counties where the materials were extracted, and to the Reclamation Fund.

4. Other Reporting

(a)   **Footnote Disclosure:** None.

(b)   **Stewardship Reporting:** None.

C.   Availability and Existence of Data

Data is available on quantities extracted and revenues received from the sale of mineral materials. However, no comprehensive value can be determined for mineral materials.

Grazing Uses

A. **Background**

1. **General Information and Legal Background**

Ownership: The United States owns Public rangelands. Agencies of the Federal Government are responsible for stewardship of the public rangelands, including managing the natural resources on the surface of the lands. Federal agencies manage approximately 255,000,000 acres of grazing lands for domestic livestock use through 10-year permits or leases (Bureau of Land Management—165 million acres, and Forest Service—90 million acres). In addition, 16 Alaska native corporations graze reindeer without charge on 5 million acres of public land managed by the BLM.

The Federal Government does not transfer ownership or control of the rangelands because the public lands are, by law, managed for multiple use (mineral development; natural, scenic, scientific, and heritage values; outdoor recreation; range; timber; watershed; and wildlife and fish) and sustained yield for future generations. By law, these lands are also managed to avoid permanent impairment of the productivity of the land and to avoid permanent impairment of the quality of the environment.

Legal Authority: Legal authority for BLM's management of the public rangelands is found in three major laws: the Taylor Grazing Act of 1934 (43 USC 315), the Federal Land Policy and Management Act of 1976 (43 USC 1752), and the Public Rangelands Improvement Act of 1978 (43 USC 1901). Other laws containing rangeland administrative authority are the Oregon and California Railroad Grant Lands Act of 1937 and Coos Bay Wagon Grant Lands (43 USC 1181d), the Bankhead-Jones Farm Tenant Act of 1937 (7 USC 1012), the Carson-Folly Act of 1968, and the Federal Noxious Weed Act of 1974 (7 USC 2801).

Alaska reindeer grazing is governed by the Reindeer Act of 1937, the Taylor Grazing Act of 1934, and the Federal Land Policy and Management Act of 1976.

Legal authority for Forest Service management of the public rangelands is found in the Organic Administration Act of 1897 (16 USC 551), the Bankhead-Jones Farm Tenant Act of 1937 (7 USC 1010), the Granger-Thye Act of 1950 (16 USC 571), the Multiple Use-Sustained Yield Act of 1960 (16 USC 528), the National Forest Management Act of 1976 (16 USC 472), the Federal Land Policy and Management Act of 1976 (43 USC 1752), and the Public Rangelands Improvement Act of 1978 (43 USC 1901). The Department of the Defense (DoD) conducts natural resources management activities under the Sikes Act, 16 USC 670. DoD legal authority to lease lands for grazing and agricultural purposes is in 10 USC 2667(d)(4).

Sale of Forage: Approximately 27,400 permittees or lessees purchase forage from the Federal Government for the use of about 30,100 grazing allotments under 10-year grazing permits or leases. The BLM administers grazing on 21,600 allotments grazed by 18,800 permittees or lessees, while the Forest Service administers grazing on 8,500 allotments grazed by 8,600 permittees.

Valuation: The current grazing fee is $1.35 per Animal Unit Month (AUM). The grazing fee for public rangeland is computed from a fee formula established by Executive Order 12548 dated February 14, 1986, and incorporated rules (36 CFR 222.50 and 43 CFR 4130.8). The formula uses a base forage value established in the 1968 Western Livestock Grazing Survey, multiplied by the weighted averages for privately owned, non-irrigated pasture or rangeland rental rates in the 11 western states, plus the average price ranchers receive for the sale of beef cattle, minus the estimated cost for producing livestock on public lands. The DoD leases lands for grazing or agriculture on a competitive base and valuation is based on fair market value. The grazing fee has varied widely from year to year depending upon market forces. The Federal Government sells an average of 17,950,000 AUMs of forage each year (BLM, 10 million AUMs, and FS, 7.95 million AUMs).

Rules governing fees for grazing use and occupancy of National Forest System lands in the eastern and southern regions are set forth at 36 CFR 222. Procedures for permits awarded noncompetitively are at 36 CFR 222.53. Competitive bidding procedures are at 36 CFR 222.54. Grazing fees charged on eastern National Forests are based on fair market value as determined by either comparable private grazing use rates adjusted for the difference in the costs of grazing comparable private lands and National Forest System lands, or by prevailing prices in competitive markets for other Federal or state leased lands.

2. Description of "Stages" for Resource

Conveyed: Permits or leases are allocated to the holders of preference base properties. Permittees or lessees own or control the base property ranches through lease to which the Federal Government assigns grazing preference and the amount of permitted grazing use. Grazing permits or leases are renewable to the preference holders for 10-year terms when the permittee or lessee has demonstrated good stewardship through compliance with the rules, terms, and conditions of the grazing permit or lease. Most of the DoD leases are for 5 years or less in accordance with statute. However, leases may be extended beyond 5 years if the Secretary of Defense determines that a lease for a longer period will promote national defense or be in the public interest.

Available for Sale: Forage is sold annually through the grazing operation described on the permit or lease. Permittees or lessees may apply to amend their annual operation and are then authorized to make the described use when approved by the government. Grazing fees are due and payable before grazing use is made.

The Government recognizes approximately 13,070,000 AUMs of forage assigned to BLM preference holders and 9,244,000 AUMs of forage to holders of Forest Service permits. Of this amount, approximately 2,200,000 AUMs are permanently suspended from use by the BLM because the forage supply is limited. There are approximately 4,326,000 AUMs of forage that are placed in temporary nonuse (3,000,000 AUMs for the BLM and 1,326,000 AUMs for the FS) each year for various reasons, including drought, fire, operators' financial ability to buy livestock, livestock disease/quarantine, or conservation improvement of rangeland resources through short-term rest from use.

Administratively and Legislatively Withdrawn: A few rangeland areas are withdrawn and devoted to other purposes that preclude livestock grazing. Before a permit or lease is canceled due to withdrawal, the preference holder is given a two-year notice. Some of the activities that preclude livestock grazing include military bombing ranges, community sanitary land fills, recreation sites and campgrounds, public land sales, and exchanges where public land becomes private or state owned.

Unknown and Undiscovered Resource: The total quantity of animal unit months of forage available for permitting/leasing is contingent upon uncontrollable environmental factors.

B. Current Reporting

1. **Asset Recognition:** The financial records of government agencies currently do not recognize forage as an asset.

2. **Revenue Recognition:** Revenue resulting from the sale of forage is recognized when lease or permit payments are collected.

3. **Cost Recognition**

   (a) **Cost of Resources Sold:** The value of forage is not matched against lease or permit revenue, as this value is not determinable.

   (b) **Cost of selling:** The cost of forage sales are borne by agency operating appropriations and are recognized in the period incurred. The DoD supplements most of the costs from lease proceeds, but may use operating appropriations if necessary.

(c)   **Cost of Management:** Rangeland management is funded through operating appropriations. Costs are recognized in the period incurred. The DoD supplements most of the costs from lease proceeds, but may use operating appropriations if necessary.

(d)   **Transfers of Revenue/Distribution of Receipts:**
BLM: Receipts from the sale of forage are distributed in accordance with Section 10 of the Taylor Grazing Act as amended by Section 401 (b) of the Federal Land Policy and Management Act. Fees collected from designated grazing districts under Section 3 of the Taylor Grazing Act are distributed as follows: 12 ½ percent to the state and county where collected, 50 percent to the managing Federal agency for on-the-ground rangeland improvement, and 37 ½ percent to the general fund of the U.S. Treasury. Fees collected from grazing lease or permits under Section 15 of the Taylor Grazing Act are distributed as follows: 50 percent to the state and county where collected and 50 percent to the managing Federal agency for on-the-ground rangeland improvement. DoD: The DoD retains all grazing and agricultural lease proceeds for lease administration, leased land improvements, and natural resource management. Forest Service: Grazing fees are collected in accordance with 43 United States Code, Section 1751, and subsequently deposited by the agency to manage and maintain range development on National Forest Systems. Fifty percent of the monies received as fees for grazing are deposited in the Treasury as miscellaneous receipts. As further directed under 36 Code of Federal Regulations, Section 222.10, the remaining fifty percent of all monies received as fees for grazing is credited to the range betterment fund to accomplish range development. Fifty percent of the monies from this fund are expended on the National Forest where the fees derived to arrest range deterioration and improve forage conditions. The remaining 50 percent of the fund are allocated within the Forest Service regions where the fees derived for rehabilitation, protection, and improvement of those National Forest lands. The Forest Service reports these transfers and distributions as costs on the Statement of Net Cost and as transfers-out on the Statement of Changes in Net Position.

4. Other Reporting

(a)   **Footnote Disclosure:** BLM & FS: None.

(b)   **Stewardship Reporting:** None

C.   Availability and Existence of Data

Data is available on the number of grazing permits/leases and the AUM's leased. Data is available on revenues generated and the distributions of lease or permit revenues. Data is available on range improvement revenues retained by agencies and the use of those revenues at the budget sub-activity, object class, and location (State) levels. Data is available to discuss the cost of range management, including the cost of permit/lease management, at the budget sub-activity, object class, and location (State) levels. However, data is not available on the overall quantity or fair market value of rangeland forage.

Electromagnetic Spectrum (Airwaves)

A.   Background

1.   General Information and Legal Background

Ownership. All sovereign nations own the rights to the electromagnetic spectrum within their boundaries. The U.S. Federal Government assigns the right to use portions of the spectrum to state and local governments and to the private sector for specific purposes. However, the Federal Government does not transfer ownership of the spectrum itself. A significant portion of the spectrum is reserved for defense and other government uses.

Legal authority. Legal authority for management of the U.S. spectrum rests with the Federal Communications Commission (FCC) for private users and State and local government users, and with the National Telecommunications and Information Administration for Federal Government users.

Sale of Licenses. Currently, private sector lessees purchase licenses for the right to use specific bands of spectrum at public auctions. The authority for conducting spectrum auctions was legislated in Omnibus Budget Reconciliation Act of 1993. Prior to auctions, the Spectrum was first given away to those who filed first for the license; and later, the licenses were awarded by lottery. Generally, the license period is ten years and the license, once granted, can be renewed and retained indefinitely unless there is substantial reason for revoking the license, such as failure to pay license fees.

The FCC currently controls the use for any given portion of the spectrum (e.g. television, cellular phone). At some point in the future, the FCC may allow licensees greater control over the use of radio frequencies.

Valuation. Over the last three years, the FCC has auctioned bands of spectrum with a sale value of more than $23 billion. Installments are permitted for payment of licenses. The FCC does not put a value on the spectrum to be sold. The market, at the time of sale, determines the value of the spectrum, and many variables contribute to the sale value. The Congressional Budget Office has estimated previous sales, however, these estimates proved to be incorrect. The usefulness and value of any portion of the spectrum is dependent on technology. Lower frequencies generally have more uses, and technological advances are expected to provide uses for higher frequencies currently considered "unusable."

2. Description of "Stages for" Resource

Conveyed

Conveyance of the spectrum takes place (a) when an auction is held to sell licenses to the private sector or (b) when portions are set aside at no cost for use by state and local governments (e.g. for use by emergency personnel). The "purchase price" paid at auctions can be significant, however, periodic license fees tend to be nominal.

Only the right to use the spectrum for a period of time is sold. The spectrum itself is not sold, and all rights revert to the government if license terms are not met. The spectrum is permanent and there is no known way in which the spectrum could be destroyed or damaged.

The government has the right to move licensees from one portion of the spectrum to another. This has been done in the past, for example to obtain a large block of the spectrum for auction to pager companies.

Available for Sale

Radio frequencies not currently under license or reserved by the Federal Government may be auctioned by the FCC under established procedures.

Administratively and Legislatively Withdrawn

The Federal Government reserves significant portions of the spectrum for use. The primary Federal use relates to national defense, however, most Federal agencies are assigned small portions of the frequency for radio communication and similar purposes.

Unknown / Undiscovered

The highest frequencies of the spectrum currently have no known use. However, technological advances continue to widen the "usable" portion of the spectrum.

B. Current Reporting

The FCC is not currently required to publish financial statements and subject them to an independent audit and as such does not do so.

C. Availability and Existence of Data

Extensive data is available regarding frequencies licensed for private sector and state and local uses, and in general what purposes those frequencies can be used for. No value can be determined for radio frequencies to be auctioned, or for the radio spectrum in its entirety. Some data related to government uses may be considered classified information.

Appendix B. Minority Comments on General Reporting Principles

The report of the FASAB Natural Resources Task Force provides useful information concerning the proper Federal accounting treatment of natural resources. However, some of the report's basic recommendations appear to fall short of providing the most useful accounting framework for management and policy making. This appendix explains those concerns.

The concerns fall into three main areas.

- First, we think that the basic concepts of SSFAS No.7 are valid, and that sales of natural resources should not offset agencies' gross costs, unless the full costs of the natural resources sold are recognized. In contrast, one alternative (*Option 2* on page 32) in the document does not promote recognition of the Government's true opportunity costs, and would enable revenue from seemingly costless asset sales to offset other costs in a manner that could encourage inefficient sales and management.

- Second, we think that it would be appropriate for some natural resource assets -- in particular, those where the asset is held for remunerative operations or sale -- to be recognized on the balance sheet, and not solely in the stewardship report. This would also allow the full costs of natural resources that are sold to be recognized on the Statement of Net Cost.

- Finally, the objective of the FASAB statements should be to develop an accounting framework that will assist program managers and policy makers in their decision making. The report raises a valid concern about the lack of good information on many Federal natural resources. Our view is that at least part of the solution to this problem is for the Government to develop basic data where it has valuable resources that it intends to sell or manage for remunerative purposes.

These concerns are discussed below.

Net Costs and SSFAS No.7

FASAB designed the Statement of Net Cost to relate the cost of operations to performance measures. To meet the operating objectives laid out in SFFAC No. 1, *Objectives of Federal Financial Reporting*, cost must be matched with the provision of goods and services to the public or other Government entities. To determine the net cost of an exchange activity -- i.e., the part of the cost that is not offset by revenue earned from the goods and services provided -- the related revenue must be matched with the cost. When this is done, the gross and net cost of an entity can be compared with its related outputs and outcomes to evaluate its operating performance, pricing policy, and economic decisions. Similarly, the net cost to the taxpayer can be estimated for the activity's related outputs provided to the public. The standards in SFFAS No. 7 therefore provide for matching exchange revenue against related cost as closely as practicable.

This ideal model breaks down when a major part of an entity's gross costs are not recognized. SFFAS No. 7 gives two examples: the rents and royalties collected by the Minerals Management Service (MMS) for natural resources on the Outer Continental Shelf and other lands, and the FCC's auction of the radio spectrum. Since the cost of the natural resource is not recognized, the Statement of Net Cost can report only a fraction of the gross cost of operations. As a result, the exchange revenue cannot be matched against the economic cost of operations and bears little relationship to the recognized cost of the entity. If the exchange revenue were subtracted from the recognized costs, the relationship between the entity's net cost of operations and its measures of performance would be distorted. It would appear as though the selling entity was very efficient in its operations, whereas it was merely disposing of Federal assets acquired for the most part by exercising sovereign powers. Our belief is that this would violate the concept of the Statement of Net Cost and undermine the reasons for instituting it.

We therefore believe that FASAB was correct in excluding such exchange revenue from the Statement of Net Cost and instead requiring it to be accounted for as a financing source in the Statement of Changes in Net Position (and, if collected on behalf of others, to be reported as a custodial activity by the collecting entity). The Statement of Net Cost is distorted less than under any other treatment, and full visibility and accountability are maintained through other basic financial statements.

Currently, most Federal natural resources do not have significant recognized costs; the one exception may be timber on land that has been reforested. The main costs that would be reflected on agencies' Statements of Net Cost, under *Option 2* (page 32), would be just the costs of holding the sales (e.g., costs of surveys) and ongoing management. *Option 2* does not include opportunity costs -- such as current cost, market value, net realizable value, or related measures of depletion -- be reported. The following sections discuss how this might be accomplished.

Economically Productive Assets and the Balance Sheet

The report notes that a key problem with showing resource costs on the balance sheet or on the Statement of Net Cost is that information is poor. For instance, for minerals for which mining patents can be issued under the 1872 law, the Government does not make an estimate of reserves prior to sale, nor does it receive information on extraction after the sale.

We realize that there are instances when it would not be cost-effective to value many Federal natural resource holdings. Nevertheless, we think there are some cases where the Government should report asset values on the balance sheet and full cost minus earned revenue on the Statement of Net Cost. These cases are characterized by the intent to use the resources in a remunerative fashion. Resources that are being kept for "stewardship" in the traditional sense of the word (e.g., in national parks or wilderness areas) would not be reported on the balance sheet but rather would be covered in the stewardship report. (While in principle one might estimate the value of such lands for recreation or wildlife habitat uses (as well as resource extraction), in practice this would not be necessary at this time, unless one is interested in comparing preservation with alternative uses.)

Some kinds of resource costs or values would be easier to estimate than others. Forest Service timber and Bureau of Land Management forage are prime examples of resources that could be placed on the balance sheet. These assets have values that can be adequately estimated with surveys, photographs, and consideration of market conditions. While it may be impractical to value all Federal timber (or forage), it could be useful to value parcels expected to be offered for sale in the next 5 to 10 years. (A five-year period would match the budget period considered under the pay-as-you-go rules of the House of Representatives; a ten-year period would match the budget period considered by the Senate.) Timber that is unlikely to be offered -- e.g., because it is in wilderness areas -- would not be reported. Conceivably OCS leases might also be reported on the balance sheet, too, so long as publishing such information does not conflict with the objective of getting market value for the leases. (While arguably such publication could sometimes reduce bids, it would probably not be biased against receipt of fair market value).

Recognizing Information Needs

The fact that existing information is poor, however, does not imply that this situation should continue. Rather, information should be improved in cases where the benefits to having that information for decision-making exceed its cost. When the government is contemplating sale of the natural resource, information on its cost and value are important to the decision and policy and would be estimable in many, if not most, cases where they are not now estimated. We agree that resources with values that cannot be estimated in a reliable and cost-effective manner should be considered in the stewardship report. The rebuttable presumption, however, should be that resources used for remunerative purposes should be reported on the balance sheet and Statement of Net Cost.

For example, if better information were available on the value of minerals and lands that are currently subject to the 1872 mining law, it is possible that Federal sales policy would change and result in higher Federal receipts. At a minimum, better estimates would inform policy makers and the public and would improve the quality of the government's financial statements. For these resources, possible information alternatives include 1) very aggregate estimates of mineral and land value based on regional surveys or 2) more detailed assessments for tracts that are sold. As noted above, to improve feasibility the focus could be on resources expected to be offered over the next 5 to 10 years, rather than all resources. We recognize one might argue that because current law allows these lands and minerals to be sold for trivial payments, researching the value of these lands would be "throwing good money after bad." While there are different views on this issue, we think it is consistent with financial accountability for there to be improved recognition of the costs and benefits of natural resource transfers.

In principle, the measure of natural resource costs could be based either on gross market value or on estimated net realizable value (estimated market value net of expected sale costs). The gross measure has the advantage of being easier to estimate and less susceptible to manipulation (such as overstatement of expected sale costs); the net measure has the advantage of recognizing that sale costs must generally be incurred to realize any receipts. To best recognize likely realizable benefits, we lean toward using the net realizable value measure. With this approach agencies would not tend to show losses from their activities, as they would if assets were valued at gross market value; rather, agencies' actual revenues from sales, minus their sale costs, would tend to equal the resources' estimated values on the balance sheet. While high estimates of sales costs could depress estimated net asset values -- and thereby enable agencies to mask inefficient sale and management practices -- agencies would also have incentives to incur actual sale costs below their estimates and thereby realize a net gain. Agencies which -- consistent with SSFAS No. 7 -- sell resources but do not report the net realizable costs and the corresponding sale revenues on the Statement of Net Cost would tend to show higher net costs (because sale costs would continue to be reported) than agencies that do report information on net realizable costs and associated revenues. Thus, there would be accounting incentives to move toward development of better information on the value of Federal resources.

The balance sheet should be based upon the same concept of the resource value or cost as the Statement of Net Cost (i.e., current cost, market value, or estimated net realizable value). While our inclination is toward estimated net realizable value, note that realizable value could be constrained by legal and regulatory limits on sale prices. Our inclination is that realizable value be based on market value, without exceptional constraints such as are present for mining or forage lands. Finally, if production (e.g., reforestation) costs are high, both gross-market and realizable value measures might understate the Government's opportunity costs. The balance sheet should show the asset value based on (net realizable) market valuation. Presumably this same value would also be reported on the Statement of Net Costs when an asset is sold; where production costs are greater than the asset's market value, this should be noted too, perhaps through use of footnotes. This treatment would be somewhat analogous with the treatment of inventory under "lower-of-cost-or-market" rules.

Attachment A. Suggested Clarifications to Existing Revenue Standard (SFFAS No. 7)

Presented below are the task force's suggested clarifications to SFFAS No. 7 that would require all natural resource revenues to be reported as a custodial activity. Proposed additions to SFFAS No. 7 are highlighted with an underline (underline) and proposed deletions are highlighted with a strike-out (strike-out.)

(paragraph numbers reference to SFFAS No. 7)

45. Under ~~exceptional~~ some circumstances, such as ~~rents and royalties on the Outer Continental Shelf,~~ revenues from the sale of most natural resources, an entity ~~recognizes virtually no costs (either during the current period or during past periods) in connection with earning revenue it collects.~~ has recognized no value on the balance sheet for an asset it sells. Thus, the entity cannot recognize a cost for the asset itself when it is sold.

   A. In such cases, even though the collecting entity incurs some management and selling costs which could be related to the revenue, the collecting entity should not offset its gross costs by such exchange revenue in determining its net cost of operations. If such exchange revenue is retained by the entity, it should be recognized as a financing source in determining the entity's operating results. If, instead, such revenue is collected on behalf of other entities (including the U.S. government as a whole), the entity that collects the revenue should account for that revenue as a custodial activity, i.e., an amount collected for others.

   B. If the collecting entity transfers the exchange revenue to other entities, similar recognition by other entities is appropriate.

      a. If the other entities to which the revenue is transferred also recognize ~~virtually no costs in connection with the Government earning the revenue~~ no value on the balance sheet for the asset which was sold, the amounts transferred to them should not offset their gross cost in determining their net cost of operations but rather should be recognized as a financing source in determining their operating results.

      b. If the other entities to which the revenue is transferred ~~do~~ have recognize~~d~~ ~~costs in connection with the Government earning the revenue~~ a value on the balance sheet for the asset which was sold, the amounts transferred to them should offset their gross cost in determining their net cost of operations.

      c. Because the revenue is exchange revenue regardless of whether related asset costs are recognized, it should be recognized and measured under the exchange revenue standards.

[Skip to 139.]

139. The only exception to the general rule occurs when the entity recognizes ~~virtually~~ no asset cost in earning the exchange revenue, as explained in the following section.

140. **Exchange revenue unrelated to recognized cost.** In ~~exceptional~~some cases, such as revenues from the sale of most natural resources, an entity ~~may recognize virtually no costs in connection with earning revenue it collects.~~ has recognized no value on the balance sheet for the asset it sells. Thus, the entity cannot recognize a cost for the asset itself when it is sold. While it may incur some management and selling costs which could be related to the revenue, it should not offset its gross costs by the revenue to determine its net cost of operations. An ~~major~~example for many years has been the Mineral Management Service (MMS) of the Department of the Interior. It manages energy ...

141. MMS does not recognize a depletion cost ~~for various reasons, including the fact that under present accounting standards~~ because the value of natural resources is not recognized as an asset. As a result, this exchange revenue cannot be matched against the economic cost of operations and bears little relationship to the recognized cost of MMS. Therefore, it should not be subtracted from MMS's gross cost in determining its net cost of operations. If it were subtracted, the relationship between MMS's net cost of operations and its measures of performance would be distorted. This distortion would likely be greater than the distortion that will occur because of not matching any of the revenue with the management and selling costs of producing it. Similarly, the net cost of operations of the Department of the Interior would likewise be more distorted than it will be because of not matching any of the revenue with management costs.

142. No changes.

143. The rents, royalties, ~~and~~ bonuses, and other receipts from the sale of natural resources which are transferred to Treasury for the General Fund or to other Government reporting entities should be recognized similarly by these recipient entities. The revenue is exchange revenue and should be recognized and measured under the exchange revenue standards. However, neither the Government as a whole nor the other recipient entities recognize the natural resources as an asset and depletion as a cost. Therefore, the revenue should not offset the cost of operations for the U.S. Government as a whole or for these entities. As in the case of MMS, offsetting cost by this revenue would distort the relationship between the net cost of operations and the measures of the performance of these entities. This distortion would likely be greater than the distortion that will occur because of not matching revenue with the management costs which are incurred. The exchange revenue should instead be a financing source in determining the operating results and change in net position.

144. ~~The Board is addressing the accounting for natural resources in a separate project. If it concludes that the value of mineral rights should be recognized as an asset and depletion as a cost, it would be~~

~~appropriate to recognize the exchange revenue from rents, royalties, and bonuses in determining the net cost of operations.~~

145. Although MMS is the most prominent case of an entity collecting exchange revenue for which it has recognizes~~d~~ ~~virtually~~ no asset cost, ~~there can be other instances.~~ all natural resources present the same situation. For example, the Federal Communications Commission collects exchange revenue from the auction of the radio spectrum. Such revenue should be accounted for in the same way as the revenue collected by MMS.

146. One respondent to the Exposure Draft asked about the meaning of the term "virtually no costs." If an entity sells scrap metal or fully depreciated equipment, the exchange revenue or gain is not related to any cost that is recognized at the time of sale. These assets are recorded on the balance sheet as having no value at the time of sale, so the gross proceeds from the sale are not offset by any remaining book vale in calculating the entity's gain. However, unlike ~~the auctions of petroleum rights or the radio spectrum~~ the sale of natural resources, costs were recognized in past periods for the purchase of the materials or the use of the equipment. Therefore, offsetting the entity's cost by its gains from sale provides a more accurate measure of its net cost of operations over time for comparison with measures of performance over time. The standard has been ~~clarified to say that the term "virtually no costs" means that virtually no costs are recognized during past periods as well as during the current period~~ reworded so that the term "virtually no cost" is not used and has been clarified to specify that the entity has recognized no value on the balance sheet for an asset it sells because the asset is reported as required supplementary stewardship information.